CHESS OPENINGS FOR BEGINNERS

Chess Openings

FOR BEGINNERS

Essential Strategies
Every Player Should Know

Jessica Era Martin

Illustrations by Collaborate Agency

**ROCKRIDGE
PRESS**

For general information on our other products and services, please contact our Customer Care Department within the United States at (866) 744-2665, or outside the United States at (510) 253-0500.

Paperback ISBN: 978-1-63807-679-7 | eBook ISBN: 978-1-63878-509-5

Manufactured in the United States of America

Interior and Cover Designer: Jennifer Hsu
Art Producer: Megan Baggott
Editor: Van Van Cleave
Production Editor: Rachel Taenzler
Production Manager: Jose Olivera

Illustrations © 2022 Collaborate Agency; author photo courtesy of Molly Wilbanks

10 9 8 7 6 5 4 3 2 1 0

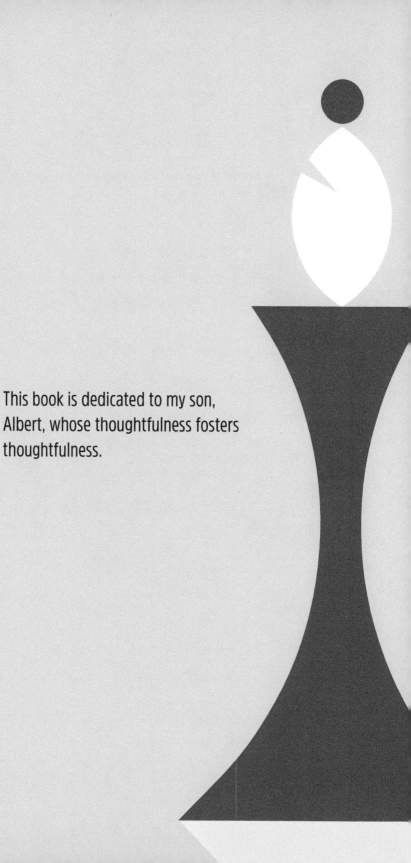

This book is dedicated to my son,
Albert, whose thoughtfulness fosters
thoughtfulness.

Contents

Introduction

Chess is one of the oldest games still played—a version of chess called Chaturanga was created in India around 600 CE! The development of opening ideas is more recent, but still about 500 to 600 years old.

Chess has always been a big part of my life. I've been playing since I was five years old, and I've been teaching and coaching for the last twenty years. Whether you are brand new or already know the basics, I'm excited to share my love and knowledge of the game with you through this book's focus on openings.

Over the centuries, openings have gone in and out of style and are continually evolving. And with the recent surge in top players using supercomputers, openings have been improved, refuted, and had novelties added. A proper understanding of this first part of the game will help you gain the confidence you need to win. There is theory galore behind many of the older openings, but this book will discuss only the Main Lines, common traps, and very basic theory so that you can understand why the pieces are placed where they are.

Additionally, this book provides a refresher on general chess rules, notation, and principles. It is integral that you become familiar with the letters and numbers associated with the board, because you will use them in notation to record and demonstrate moves. In part 2, you'll find 25 openings for beginners, and in part 3, there is a challenge section to quiz yourself on what you've learned. (You can check your answers at the back of the book.)

When you finish this book, you will have a complete introduction to a plethora of openings that you can choose from or respond to effectively in your games. And, remember, even though chess is inherently a competitive game, it is also beautiful, exciting, and fun!

PART I

Understanding Chess Openings

In this part, you will be introduced to the importance of the opening and what it means. You'll also review the basic rules of chess, including terms to know and notation to prepare you for the next part of the book. To get you started, you'll find five general opening principles and five common opening tactics explained.

CHESS OPENINGS, DEFINED

The *opening* is the beginning of the game. It's defined by how the pawns and pieces are brought out by each player, and it creates the structure for the dynamics of the middle game. In general, once players have castled (learn more on page 12), the middle game begins. The endgame is sometimes not reached because checkmate (see page 13) can occur in the middle game, but when it is, the endgame is determined by the limited number of pieces remaining on the board. Usually, once the queens have come off the board, it's an endgame. An opening can be up to 25 moves long, but this book will focus on learning just the starting moves.

Since white moves first in chess, white gets to pick the opening move. However, black has many ways of responding. The goal for both sides is to get their pieces to optimal squares where they have range or scope, and get castled. By choosing a strong opening, you'll be able to take initiative, which can often determine the result of the game. If you give your pieces the chance to attack, you'll discover more opportunities to do so in the middle game. The desperation your opponent will feel if they are unfamiliar with your opening will increase your confidence and improve your play. Also, if you're playing on a chess clock (most online games are timed), knowing some openings means you will not waste time trying to figure out what to play, because you'll already recognize the ideas and the moves. Openings aren't everything in chess, but starting the game with a *book* opening (one that's been studied for years), and not something you're guessing at, will result in more wins. This book will feature openings for both white and black, tips for both sides, and whether an opening is recommended to follow or avoid.

TERMS TO KNOW

Familiarize yourself with the following commonly used words.

Defense: An opening for black.

Develop: Bring out the pieces from the back rank.

Fianchetto: The bishop develops to the longest diagonal of the board, by landing one diagonal square from the corner (for example, g2, b2, g7, or b7).

Files: The vertical columns on a chessboard.

Gambit: Sacrificing a pawn in the opening for gain of center control or early attack.

Luft: "Air" for the king, an escape square he might run to after castling that isn't the corner; created by pushing a pawn forward, usually at the edge of the board.

Main Line: The main and most solid moves commonly played by the greatest number of people.

Material: The pieces.

Ranks: The horizontal rows on a chessboard.

Sideline: A deviation from the Main Line; a move that is not as commonly played.

System: A setup you can create against almost anything your opponent does.

Variation: Nomenclature for each way the opening can be continued; can be Main Line or sideline.

A QUICK REFRESHER ON GAME PLAY

Even if you already know the basic rules of chess, it's worth reviewing them to help you understand the strategies in this book. Certain rules, such as en passant and castling, are complicated, so take a moment to read the following section.

The Pieces

In a chess game, a player controls either the black or white pieces, and each piece is useful in its own way. The pieces are generally assigned a numerical value to help decide which exchanges are beneficial and guide strategy. (These "points" are not tallied or kept at the end of the game; checkmate always wins!) Note that you take turns in chess, there is no "passing," and you can capture only one piece at a time. Read on to learn more about each piece, ordered from lowest value to highest.

Pawn

Number per player: 8 • **Relative value:** 1 point each

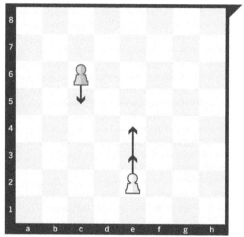

Movement: Pawns always move forward. On their first move, they may advance one or two squares. After that, they may only move one step at a time. If they reach the other side of the board, they can promote into a different piece (see Promotion, page 6).

Captures: Pawns capture diagonally one square forward. They are the only pieces that capture differently than they move. Another variation of their diagonal capture is called *en passant* (see En Passant, page 6).

Role in strategy: Pawns create the structure that determines where your pieces will go. Additionally, pawn moves are committal, because they never go backward.

EN PASSANT

This French term means "in passing." If an opponent's pawn advances past your pawn's normal diagonal capture square, resulting in it landing on a position directly next to yours, you can still take it using this special rule. To determine if you can capture using en passant, ask yourself if your pawns are side by side and if their pawn moved two squares immediately prior to your move. If yes to both, you may capture by moving diagonally forward and simply removing the adjacent pawn. The pawn will disappear automatically if you make this capture online. If you want to use en passant, you must do so on the turn immediately following your opponent's pawn push or you will lose the opportunity for that particular capture.

PROMOTION

When a pawn reaches the other side of the board, it can *promote*, which means it turns into your choice of a queen, rook, bishop, or knight. It cannot become another king and cannot remain a pawn. Promotion generally occurs in the endgame. Most of the time, you'll promote into a queen because she is the most powerful piece. Notably, on some rare occasions, you may want to "underpromote" your pawn, or turn it into a rook, bishop, or knight. This is a useful move if you need to avoid a stalemate (more on that later).

Knight

Number per player: 2 • **Relative value:** 3 points each

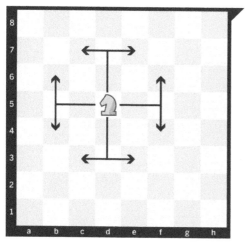

Movement: The knight moves in capital "L" shapes, two squares in one direction and one more in a perpendicular direction. The "L" shape can face any direction, including backward (upside down or sideways "L"s are okay). Additionally, it's the only piece that can jump over other pieces, both black and white.

Captures: Knights capture the piece they land on at the end of their jump. They do not capture anything along the way.

Role in strategy: Knights are sneaky and great at attacking two pieces at once in the "L" shape, known as a *fork* (page 21).

Bishop

Number per player: 2 • **Relative value:** 3 points each (some people say 3.25 to signify that a bishop is of slightly more value than a knight, though this evaluation depends on the position)

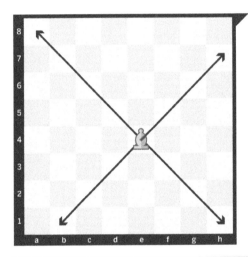

Movement: The bishop can go any number of squares it wants diagonally. Each bishop stays on its color squares; they are distinguished by calling them *dark-squared* or *light-squared*.

Captures: Same as movement.

Role in strategy: Bishops are excellent at attacking from a distance; like rooks and queens, they are long-range pieces. They're also great at making pins.

Rook

Number per player: 2 · **Relative value:** 5 points each

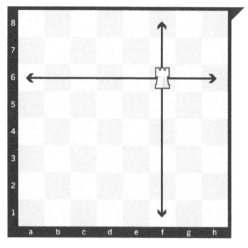

Movement: Rooks travel along files and ranks as far as they want, including backward.

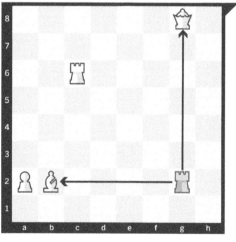

Captures: Same as movement.

Role in strategy: Rooks usually become active in the middle game once there are open files (no pawns in the way). The rook is a great attacking piece, especially when it works with a queen or another rook. Besides open files, rooks love doubling up, making pins (see page 21), and attacking the seventh rank.

Queen

Number per player: 1 (Some chess sets have an extra queen in the bag. Save this for pawn promotion!)
• **Relative value:** 9 points

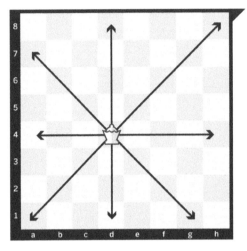

Movement: The queen moves along files, ranks, and diagonals as far as she wants. The queen doesn't jump but can move backward.

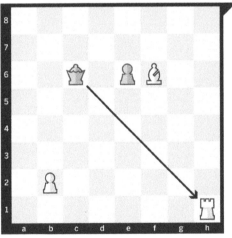

Captures: Same as movement.

Role in strategy: The queen is the best attacking piece. She's great at attacking multiple pieces at once and, most important, at checkmating. She'd rather not hang back and protect pawns, but be careful not to develop her too early, or she'll get kicked around by the other pieces.

King

Number per player: 1 • **Relative value:** The whole game!

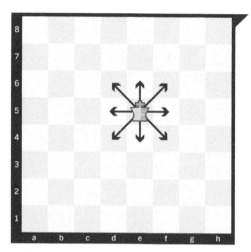

Movement: One square in any direction. However, the king legally can't move into a square that puts him in danger.

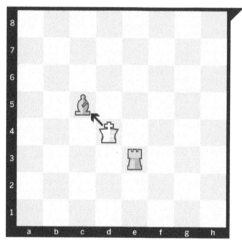

Captures: Same as legal movement. In the illustration to the left, the king can capture the bishop, but it is illegal to capture the rook, because then the king will still be in check by the bishop.

Role in strategy: Always protect your king. One way to do this is to castle (see page 12). In the endgame, the king becomes a fighting piece and can help attack pawns or shepherd a pawn up to its promotion square.

CASTLING

Castling is a unique move that helps you protect your king by getting him out of the center of the board. When castling, the king goes two squares toward either rook (kingside or queenside) and, in the same turn, your rook jumps over the king and lands directly next to him. You may only castle if these five conditions are met:

→ There are no pieces in between your king and rook

→ Your king and rook have not yet moved

→ You are not currently in check

→ You do not land in check

→ You do not "go through" check (in other words, since the king travels two squares to castle, you may not be in check at any point along that path)

Please note that you can only castle once in a game, and it's best to try to do so as soon as possible.

Checkmate, Stalemate, and Other Draws

Checkmate is how you win the game. It means that the king is in check (danger) and there is no safe way to move, block, or capture to escape from check. When you make a checkmate, the game ends. It is customary to bow or shake hands and say, "Good game!"

Some games end in what's called a *draw*—a tie between players, irrespective of who has more points or pieces at the time of the draw. Draws, like checkmates, can occur at any stage of the game, but they most commonly happen in the middle- or endgame. The five most common draws include:

1. **Stalemate:** This occurs when the king is not in danger but cannot move anywhere legally, nor can any other piece move. It usually occurs when the winning side doesn't know how to make a checkmate and accidentally traps the king *without* putting him into check.

2. **Threefold Repetition:** To prevent players from repeating a position endlessly, there is a rule in chess whereby a game ends in a draw if *both* players have moved into the same position three times (not just one player going back and forth). The moves do not have to occur consecutively, but the position does have to be the same three distinct times.

3. **Insufficient Mating Material:** There are not enough pieces to make a checkmate happen. If both sides have only a king remaining, that's an automatic draw.

4. **50-Move Rule:** This also prevents a game from going on forever. If you don't know the technique for checkmating with certain pieces and you just dance around the board forever, without moving a pawn or capturing a piece, the game ends in a draw. If a pawn is pushed on move 49, the counting begins at 1 again. A complete move is both white's and black's turn.

5. **Agreement:** You can offer or accept a draw offer if you feel you are in a slightly worse position than your opponent. However, the fighting spirit will teach you more about the game.

Remember, a draw is better than a loss, so don't give up!

HOW TO READ AND WRITE NOTATION

Writing down a chess game in its entirety can sound daunting, but there is a specific and easy language called *algebraic notation* to make it simple. Notation allows for the ability to replay historic games. Write down your moves (online it's done for you) so you can review and analyze for mistakes.

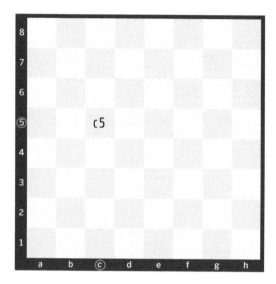

The following letters stand in for each piece:

King	K
Queen	Q
Rook	R
Bishop	B
Knight	N
Pawn	Blank; no capital letter at all

To track specific moves, write down the letter for the piece, followed by the square name that it lands on. For example: Nf3 means the knight has moved to the square f3.

1. Nf3

If two pieces can go to the same square, indicate the starting position of either the file or the rank that is different for that piece.

In this game, Grandmaster (GM) Shakhriyar Mamedyarov played 12. Rfe1 here.

When a move results in a capture, check, or checkmate, special notations are added. Castling uses different notation as well. Review the following chart to learn these specific symbols:

Any piece (except a pawn) makes any capture	x (in between the piece and square, e.g., Bxf6)
Pawn captures a piece	lowercase letter for the file the pawn starts on, x for captures, square it lands on (e.g., cxd4). If a pawn captures another pawn, you can also just write the lower-case letters the pawn starts and lands on (e.g., cd).
Check	+ (after the notation, e.g., Re1+)
Checkmate	# (after the notation, e.g., Qf7#)
Castles kingside	0-0
Castles queenside	0-0-0
Promotion	= (e.g., e8=Q)
Black's move when white's move is not listed	. . .

ANNOTATIONS

You may notice a question mark or exclamation mark after certain moves in this book. Those annotations are added after the game during analysis to indicate a good move (!) or a bad move (?). It's against tournament rules to annotate during the game, however.

FIVE GENERAL OPENING PRINCIPLES

There are certain things to keep in mind at the start of every game, and you will notice every opening incorporates these ideas.

1. Control the Center

Attack or occupy the middle of the chessboard. The four center squares are e4, d4, e5, and d5. You will want at least one of your pawns to be in the center and your knights to aim at the center. Because both players are fighting for the center early, it's difficult to achieve complete control, but the center is where all the action should be focused during the opening.

2. Build Your Pawn Structure

The way your pawns are placed is called the *pawn structure*. Certain pawn structures are more beneficial than others. For example, a pawn wall is when two pawns are side by side, creating a wall, where if your opponent lands on any of the four squares in front of your pawns, you can capture them if you want. A pawn chain is a diagonal line of pawns (at least two, usually three) with each protecting the one in front of it. The base of the pawn chain is the weakest.

Be careful not to isolate a pawn, which is when there are no pawns on either file next to it. An isolated pawn will become a target, as it can be guarded only by a bigger piece. And don't play checkers if you're playing chess: If you place all your pawns on one color, there will be huge weaknesses on the color squares they don't attack.

3. Develop Your Pieces

You must use all your back rank pieces to fabricate any type of formidable attack. Bring out your knights first, toward the center, where they have more options for movement than at the edge of the board. In general, you'll develop the kingside pieces first, because there are fewer of them in between your king and rook, allowing you to castle more quickly. Bring out more back rank pieces than pawns. If you're ever not sure what to do, look at your pieces and see if any still need to be developed.

4. Protect Your King

Your king is the only piece that does not want to remain in the center. This makes sense considering all the other pieces being developed there. The way to protect your king in the opening is to castle early. You can castle kingside or queenside but try to castle within the first 10 moves of the game. Make luft if you need to.

5. Connect Your Rooks

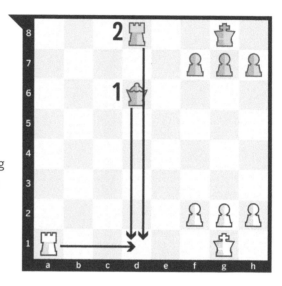

Once you've developed your knight and bishop, and have castled, the way to connect your rooks is to develop the queen and any remaining minor pieces so that the rooks are on the same rank, with no pieces in between. This ensures two things: Neither rook will be hanging, and the back rank is less likely to succumb to an opposing rook coming down the board to checkmate your king. If only one rook is guarding the back rank (or if both have left), and if you haven't made luft, your opponent conceivably could create a checkmate on the edge of the board where your king is. (This is called a *back rank checkmate*.)

TACTICS

A *tactic* is a short-term trick that enables you to force a win of material or the game. Tactics are different from *strategies*, in that strategies are longer-term plans that improve your position but may not immediately win you a piece. Tactics can occur in any stage of the game, and good positions provide opportunities for tactical combinations. Following are five tactics you will encounter in this book.

1. Hanging Pieces/ Counting

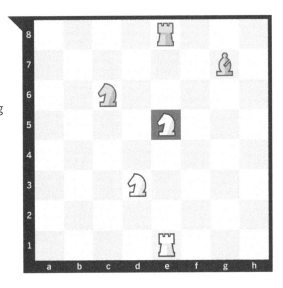

Remember, each piece has a value, and you want to capture anything that is unprotected, or *hanging*. A piece is also considered hanging if its value is greater than the piece attacking it. You're almost always going to capture a queen with a less valuable piece (unless it leads to you getting checkmated). For example, you would capture a queen even if you lose a rook: The queen is worth 9 and the rook 5, so you will have a material advantage.

In chess, if there are more attacking pieces on a certain piece than there are defenders, that piece will be hanging. And after all those exchanges, you will be up material. If there are an equal number of attackers and defenders, the piece is considered safe, or not hanging. This is called *counting attackers and defenders*. It's simpler to count than to calculate what would happen after all the exchanges.

2. Forks and Double Attacks

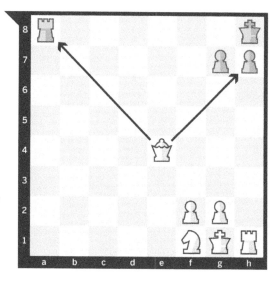

A *fork* is when one piece attacks two. Make sure to attack pieces that are hanging and that can't attack back. A *double attack* is when one piece aims at two things; for example, a hanging piece and a checkmate square. The best thing about forks and double attacks is that even though your opponent can move one piece out of the way, you'll get one of the pieces or squares you want.

3. Pin

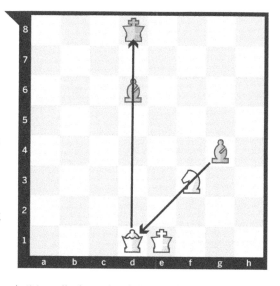

A *pin* involves three pieces in a straight line (file, rank, or diagonal). You have the piece in front, whereas your opponent has the middle and back pieces. The piece in the middle can't or shouldn't move because it needs to block the more valuable piece behind. If the back piece is a king (and therefore the middle piece can't move), it is called an *absolute pin*. A *relative pin* is one where the middle piece doesn't want to move, because then the piece behind it will be captured.

Sometimes you don't want to capture the pinned piece (if it's worth fewer points than the piece you're using to capture it). In that case, you can try to put pressure on it. Pressure simply means you attack the pinned piece again with another piece. Since it can't move, you have time to bring another piece into the attack. This way, you'll have more attackers on the pinned piece than your opponent has defenders, and you can win material. Also note, because it can't move, a pinned piece does not protect.

4. Discovered Attack/Check

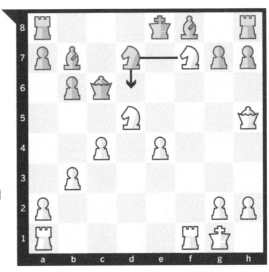

Discoveries are also long-range, three-piece attacks. However, this time, the piece in the middle is yours, not your opponent's. When you move the piece in the middle, your piece behind it makes the attack against the opponent's back piece. A discovered check means that when you move the piece in the middle, your piece behind it will suddenly be giving check. This gives your middle piece immunity to move basically anywhere safely, since the opponent's following turn must be used to get out of check. The discovered double check, when both the piece that moves and the piece behind it attack the opponent's king, is the most forcing move in chess.

5. Remove the Guard

This is a super fun tactic. You want something, but it's being protected? Eliminate the piece that's guarding what you want. Then capture the newly hanging piece, or make your checkmate as in the following example.

After removing the knight, h7 can be safely captured!

HOW TO CHOOSE AN OPENING

There are hundreds of openings and variations, and this book demonstrates 25 openings everyone should know, so you will have lots of choices for picking a few favorites. Following are some ideas to consider when selecting which to play.

1. Whom are you playing against?

If your opponent is a beginner, you might try a more aggressive line with lots of sneaky traps, such as the Fried Liver Attack. If you know they are a strong player, use what you feel most comfortable with. If you aren't sure of their skill level, go for the most solid opening, as opposed to a gambit or risky opening. Gambits and sidelines are popular at the club level because they often trick people into falling for a tactic and losing material or the game. Generally, gambits are not recommended at the higher levels because no one will fall for the trick, and then you are left in a worse position throughout the remainder of the game. How you practice is how you perform; therefore, I recommend learning and practicing solid lines, and not the offshoots or dubious openings.

2. What most closely aligns with your style of play?

If you are more of a positional and strategic player, you might choose a d4 opening for white, or the Caro-Kann defense for black. If you like more dynamic play and are more tactical, play 1. e4 for white, and the Sicilian for black.

3. Have you tried out all the openings?

Play through all the openings in this book at least once and try out the ones that resonate with you in your games with friends or online. Your goal is to know a handful of openings well, not to know every single possible line by heart. At this stage of your chess career, that's completely unnecessary (and much too daunting a task).

4. What do you enjoy and why?

In general, you should play what you enjoy, whether you like an opening because it makes sense to you, has lots of traps, feels safe, or feels appropriately risky; whenever you are playing something you enjoy, your confidence is boosted. That's important for playing good moves.

PART II

Essential Openings to Know

In this section, you will learn twenty-five of the most important openings in chess. Some will be for white and others for black, though all diagrams show white playing at the bottom and black on top for consistency. I will provide the introduction to these openings, including the Main Line (the most played move order), and top variations if critical. Look for tips on how to set or avoid traps and practice each opening on your own chessboard. Once you feel comfortable with an opening, try it out on your friends or a free site such as Chess.com or Lichess.org.

SCHOLAR'S MATE

Although this opening is not played at the top levels because it is easily refuted, it is an opening trap that everyone should know. In it, white aims to open lines for their bishop and queen and target the weak f7 square. In large part, this opening is just a trick, but it is one you must be prepared to stop.

■ SCHOLAR'S MATE MOVES ■

1. e4	e5
2. Qh5	Nc6
3. Bc4	If Nf6??
4. Qxf7#	

The first thing to notice as white is that the f7 square is defended only by black's king. Note also that f7 is a light square, meaning that it is best attacked by long-range, light-squared pieces. How can you prepare such an attack? With your go-to 1. e4, now you've just opened the bishop and queen.

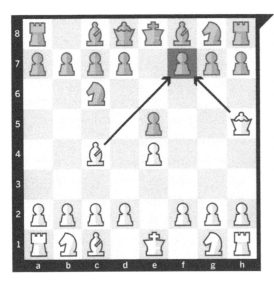

Black can play 1 . . . e5, then white brings their queen out with 2. Qh5, pinning the pawn on f7 and attacking black's hanging pawn on e5. Black should guard the pawn with 2 . . . Nc6. Obviously, if the queen immediately takes on f7, she will just get captured. So, you add an attacker with 3. Bc4. Now there's a real threat!

For white to complete the Scholar's Mate, black must make a blunder on move 3 by not blocking the queen or protecting f7 again. There are lots of ways to go wrong here. A natural-looking and super common move at the beginner level, 3 . . . Nf6??, allows white to swoop in on f7 with 4. Qxf7#.

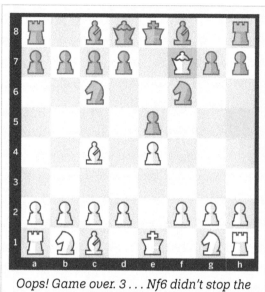

Oops! Game over. 3 . . . Nf6 didn't stop the checkmate on f7.

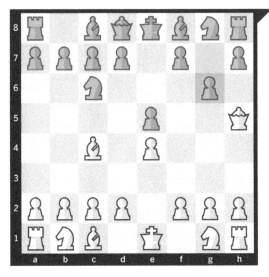

Instead, Black should play 3 . . . g6 (if e5 is guarded) or 3 . . . Qe7 to protect the pawn on f7 again.

After avoiding the Scholar's Mate, black's next goal is to castle; note that after black castles, f7 is guarded by the rook. Protecting f7 by putting the knight on the edge of the board is not recommended because white can play a move such as d3 or d4 to discover an attack on the knight on h6 (by the bishop on c1), and once again black is in trouble. White's plan is to remove the guard, and then play Qxf7#. Remember: "Knights on the rim are dim!"

Plans for white: White can also try this opening by placing the queen on f3 instead of h5, as it still attacks f7. Or you can bring the bishop out to c4 first, and then the queen.

Plans for black: Black can try the same trick on white by focusing on the target square f2. Always keep an eye on f7 at the start of every game. Continue to develop with this in mind.

GIUOCO PIANO, OR THE ITALIAN GAME

Analyzed for hundreds of years, the Giuoco Piano opening was first mentioned in the Göttingen manuscript, the very first chess book, written about 1500 CE. The Italian is one of the quickest ways to castle and aims at the weakest square on the board, f7. It has never gone out of style, largely due to its plentiful tactical opportunities for white.

■ GIUOCO PIANO MOVES ■

1. e4	e5
2. Nf3	Nc6
3. Bc4	

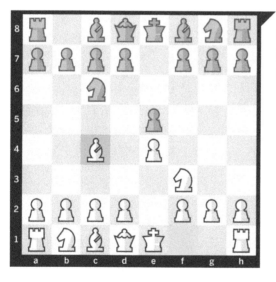

White's key move is bringing out the "Italian bishop" to c4, which aims at both the center and f7.

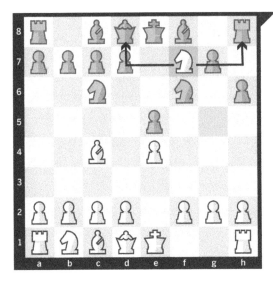

If black plays 3 . . . Nf6 you have 4. Ng5 *also* aiming at f7! Black must play 4 . . . d5, otherwise you will likely play 5. Nxf7 and fork the queen and the rook. Note that the king wouldn't be able to take because the knight would be guarded by white's bishop on c4.

Main Line, or Giuoco Pianissimo

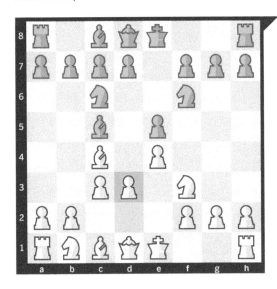

After the recommended move for black, 3 . . . Bc5, white will play 4. c3. The purpose of this pawn move is to prepare for an eventual d4 push. Black plays 4 . . . Nf6 to attack white's e-pawn and develop a piece toward the center. The most common move for white is 5. d3, which protects e4.

Black can now play 5 . . . d6 or 5 . . . a6. White has several choices, but the most principled is to castle.

Variation: Center Attack

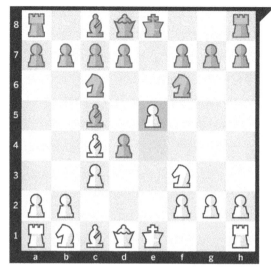

White may also play 5. d4 instead of the quieter 5. d3. Black captures, 5 . . . ed, and white plays the *intermezzo* ("in-between" move) 6. e5, which attacks the knight on f6.

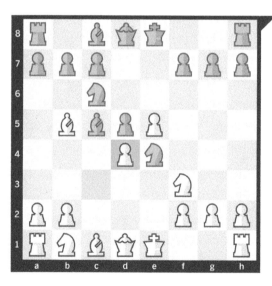

Black counterattacks with 6 . . . d5, aiming at white's bishop, and white saves the bishop with 7. Bb5, which pins the knight on c6. Black saves the knight by moving to e4, and white finally captures the pawn on d4.

Plans for white: Always keeping an eye on f7, white will castle early, and they have ideas of playing Bg5 to pin the knight to black's queen. White can develop the knight to d2, play Re1, then Nf1, and from there the knight eyes both e3 and g3. The queenside knight will become a kingside attacker. There are loads of tactics on f7 due to white's bishop on c4 pinning the pawn after black castles kingside.

Plans for black: Black tries to hold on to their dark-squared bishop as it will pin the pawn on f2 after white castles. Sometimes this means playing moves like . . . a6 and . . . Ba7 to hide. The bishop exerts a lot of pressure along the diagonal to the king. Black castles kingside and might try for . . . Nh5 and . . . Qf6 in the Pianissimo. In all lines, it's a fight for the center, and both sides bring their pieces to the kingside to attack.

FRIED LIVER ATTACK

Yes, that's really what it's called! The Fried Liver comes from the Two Knights Variation in the Italian Game. It was first played in Rome circa 1600 CE. It can be devastating for black as there are many ways to go wrong. This opening is not often played at the very top levels, but it is instructive at the novice level because it shows you how to attack quickly.

■ FRIED LIVER ATTACK MOVES ■

1. e4	e5
2. Nf3	Nc6
3. Bc4 (Italian)	Nf6
4. Ng5	d5
5. ed	

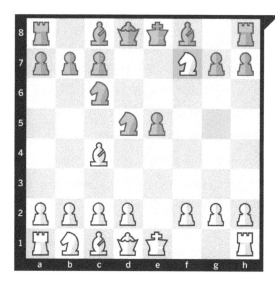

Here's where it gets fun. Black's most natural-looking move 5 . . . Nxd5 is no good because of the following trick. (Instead, play 5 . . . Na5 to save your knight.) After 5 . . . Nxd5 white can sacrifice and attack ("sac and attack") with 6. Nxf7!

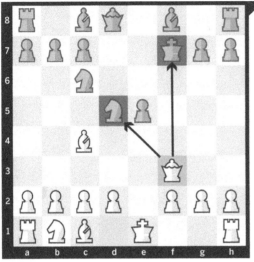

Even though the bishop isn't guarding white's knight on f7, they sacrifice to bring the king out, and now black has to play 6 . . . Kxf7. White then mounts a double attack on the knight and king with 7. Qf3+. Note that black's knight cannot block the check and save himself because he is pinned by white's bishop.

At this point, black has a major blunder to avoid: the awful 7 . . . Kg8. This is mate for white along the diagonal by taking on d5. Black can throw in a bishop to block for a second, but white takes it, and the game is over.

Instead, black can try 7 . . . Ke6, which holds on to the knight. The knight is still pinned, however, and white can put pressure on it with 8. Nc3. Black is still losing; it will be easy for white to find attacking moves with black's king in the center of the board.

Plans for white: The Fried Liver is a tactical frenzy targeting open lines and f7. Don't worry about material as much as your initiative and bringing in all your pieces to attack the king. Castling will help you develop your rook toward the center, and you can play Re1 next. Moves such as d4 will come in handy to open the center and develop your dark-squared bishop.

Plans for black: After 5. ed, you must move your c6 knight. Try 5 . . . Na5 to attack the bishop on c4. Do not capture d5 with your knight.

RUY LÓPEZ, OR THE SPANISH

This is one of the oldest openings in chess history! A Spanish priest named Ruy López de Segura published a chess book in 1561 naming the opening. Because it's been played for hundreds of years, there are countless variations. It can be played by any skill level and is the most common opening chosen by Grandmasters (GMs). The goal for white is to attack the center and undermine control of black's center. White develops the kingside quickly and is therefore able to castle right away.

■ **RUY LÓPEZ MOVES** ■

1. e4	e5
2. Nf3	Nc6
3. Bb5	

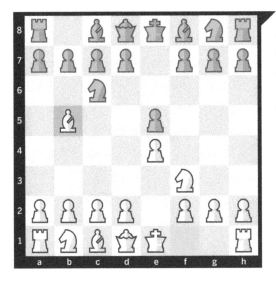

The e-pawns come out first, attacking the center and preventing an immediate pawn wall (because the e-pawns will capture another pawn on d or f). White's knight develops and attacks the center pawn with 2. Nf3. Black's best way of guarding this pawn is with their knight, so as not to block any other pieces (2 . . . Nc6), then white plays 3. Bb5. Black has many ways to respond. Let's look at the Main Line, also called the Morphy Defense, first.

Main Line: Morphy Defense

After white brings out the bishop, black plays 3 . . . a6 to kick the bishop back. In this defense, white retreats the bishop with 4. Ba4. Black plays 4 . . . Nf6, attacking the center, and white castles on move 5.

Castling leaves white's e4 pawn hanging temporarily. But capturing it while black's king is in the center can make white's attacking plan simple after opening the center further with d4.

You may be wondering why white's bishop doesn't take the knight on c6. That's because after black captures back with their d-pawn, opening their queen and bishop, if white takes the pawn on e5, which is now hanging, black can play . . . Qd4, attacking both the pawn and the knight (a fork!), and winning back the pawn. Black's resulting position is slightly better, so this move is not advised for white.

Variation: Main Line Closed

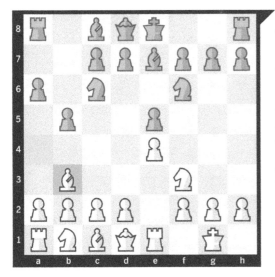

After white castles, the Main Line for black is 5 . . . Be7. This is called the Closed Variation because black does not capture the pawn on e4, opening the center. White plays 6. Re1 to guard the e-pawn. Now the threat of capturing the knight on c6 is real. So black should play 6 . . . b5 to kick the bishop back again. White retreats to a very nice diagonal, and the only one available, 7. Bb3. The bishop then aims at f7, which is black's weakest square.

Plans for white: Gain space in the center with a properly timed d4 push. It will need to be prepared with c3 and h3. The c-pawn replaces the d-pawn that's just been captured while the move h3 prevents black's bishop from coming to g4 and pinning the knight to the queen. Often white's queenside knight will maneuver from b1-d2-f1-g3 and attack the kingside.

Plans for black: Black still needs to castle. They can do so now or play . . . d6 first and then castle. The most popular variation currently is the Marshall Attack: After 7. Bb3, black castles 7 . . . 0-0, white plays 8. c3 (to prepare d4) and black strikes in the center with 8 . . . d5. This aggressive gambit takes advantage of white's underdeveloped queenside. Black will likely fianchetto the queenside bishop and go for a quick attack.

FOUR KNIGHTS GAME

This ancient opening is fairly quiet and therefore has been less popular at the top levels. You may encounter it at novice levels, as it employs the principle of developing your knights toward the center.

■ **FOUR KNIGHTS GAME MOVES** ■

1. e4	e5
2. Nf3	Nc6
3. Nc3	Nf6

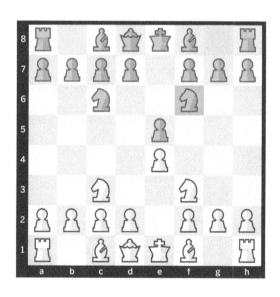

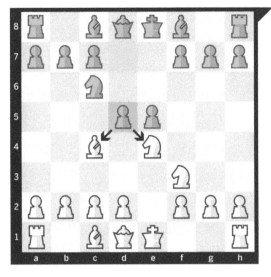

On move 4, you may be tempted to play the natural-looking 4. Bc4. Don't do it. This leads to the Center Fork Trick, where black will capture with 4 . . . Nxe4, and after 5. Nxe4, black has 5 . . . d5 forking the knight and bishop. Black wins the material back and gains a slightly better position. Instead, try the Spanish or Scotch Variations below.

Variation: Spanish

The move 4. Bb5 leads to the Four Knights Game: Spanish Variation. You may notice that this opening reminds you of the Ruy López (page 38).

Variation: Scotch

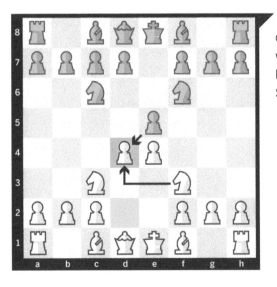

On move 4, white can also play 4. d4 in what is aptly called the Four Knights Game: Scotch Variation.

Plans for white: White develops the bishops and castles kingside. Play may continue on any side of the board. Because there are no imbalances, the opening can lead to a symmetrical, drawish position.

Plans for black: In the Spanish Variation, black literally copies white's moves after 4. Bb5 with 4 . . . Bb4. Then white castles, black castles, white plays d3, and black plays . . . d6 (called, unsurprisingly, Double Spanish Variation). In all lines, black will castle kingside and develop pieces to typical squares.

SCOTCH GAME

A quick attack in the center with pawns defines the Scotch Game. It was first written about in 1750 by the Italian Master Ercole del Rio. But the Scotch didn't get its name until 1824 when, in a famous match between London and Edinburgh, the Scots won 2.5 out of 3 of the games played using this opening. Although less common than the Ruy López or the Italian, the Scotch is a great way to learn how to immediately attack the center of the board with a pawn wall on e4 and d4.

■ **SCOTCH GAME MOVES** ■

1. e4	e5
2. Nf3	Nc6
3. d4	ed
4. Nxd4	

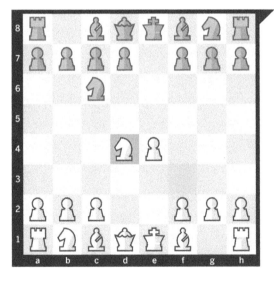

There are quite a few variations, but the top two moves are 4 . . . Nf6, the Schmidt Variation, and 4 . . . Bc5, the Classical Variation.

Variation: Schmidt, Mieses

After 4 ... Nf6, try continuing with the Mieses Variation— 5. Nxc6—which scores well for white. Black cannot take 5 ... dxc6 without prompting a queen trade, losing the right to castle, and having doubled pawns in the endgame. Instead, black plays 5 ... bxc6 and, now that white has removed the knight from c6, they can play 6. e5, kicking the knight on f6.

Black can then play 6 ... Qe7, pinning the pawn, and white must play 7. Qe2 to unpin. After 7 ... Nd5, white kicks the knight again with 8. c4, and white will enjoy more central space.

Variation: Classical

With 4 . . . Bc5, note that black develops the bishop with tempo, because they are also attacking the knight again. White can defend with tempo by responding with 5. Be3. Black then adds a third attacker with 5 . . . Qf6.

How does white guard the knight again?

White must play 6. c3, and now there are three attackers and three defenders on the knights, meaning it is safe, not hanging. Another more aggressive way to play the Classical is to take black's knight with 5. Nxc6, instead of guarding their own. Just don't get mated if black brings out the queen, threatening f2: 5 . . . Qf6.

Play 6. Qe2 and you'll be fine.

Plans for white: Try to grab and maintain space in the center of the board. If your bishop can get to c4, you may be able to find tricks on f7. Castling is delayed in this opening, but don't forget to do it.

Plans for black: If white takes on c6, generally you will capture back with your b-pawn, unless your queen has already developed so there won't be an early queen trade on d8. There are some sharp pins in these variations due to the open lines. Black will castle kingside eventually.

FRENCH DEFENSE

This opening, which became popular in the 1800s, is named after a correspondence match between London and Paris. Although it is not as popular as 1 . . . c5, the Sicilian Defense (page 54), or 1 . . . e5, it nevertheless is a solid and important opening to know.

■ **FRENCH DEFENSE MOVES** ■

1. e4	e6
2. d4	d5

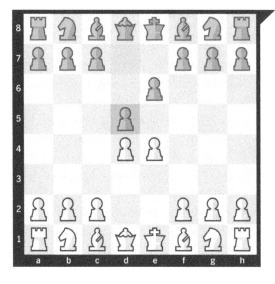

White has several choices for move 3, including 3. Nc3 (most common) and 3. Nd2. When considering black's next move, note that there are pros and cons to the pawns being on white squares. On the one hand, pushing the e-pawn allows the dark-squared bishop to develop, and placing it on e6 means if white were ever to put a bishop on c4, the effect of that bishop would be blunted, since the pawn would prevent it from directly aiming at f7. It does block in the light-squared bishop, however, which can lead to a more cramped position for black.

Variation: Winawer

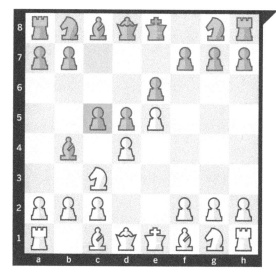

After white plays 3. Nc3, black can choose the Winawer with 3 . . . Bb4. This move pins the knight, meaning e4 is undefended again. White plays 4. e5, the Advance Winawer Variation, to make a pawn chain, and black must play 4 . . . c5 to strike at it. For now, the position is closed.

Variation: Classical

After 3. Nc3, black can also choose the Classical Variation with 3 . . . Nf6. The black knight puts more pressure on e4, so now there are two attackers and only one defender (the knight on c3). White will play either 4. Bg5, which pins the knight, or push 4. e5, attacking the knight.

Variation: Tarrasch

On move 3, white can also choose 3. Nd2, the Tarrasch Variation, which avoids the Winawer, because if black tries to pin the knight now with 3 . . . Bb4, white can simply play 4. c3, kicking the bishop back.

Variation: Advance

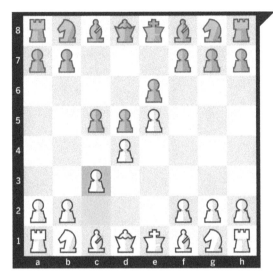

On move 3, white can also simply play e5, the Advance Variation, attacking the f6-square where black's knight would have liked to have gone. Now black must play 3 . . . c5, which hits the base of white's pawn chain. White protects d4 by increasing the pawn chain with 4. c3.

Plans for white: In most lines, white will enjoy extra space in the center and attack on the kingside. There are lots of tactics on h7 after black eventually castles in the lines where white has pushed a pawn to e5, because that pawn prevents the black knight from remaining on f6, where it would naturally defend h7.

Plans for black: In the Winawer, black often trades their bishop for the knight, after white plays a3, and plays the imbalance where white has two bishops but also doubled pawns. In the Advance Variation, black will focus their attention on the d4 pawn, with moves such as . . . Nc6 and . . . Qb6. In all lines, black must fight for the center with a pawn break on c5. Castling is delayed, and often black will attack the queenside.

CARO-KANN DEFENSE

This is a very solid opening, first analyzed at length by Horatio Caro and Marcus Kann in the 1800s. Its defining move is black playing 1 . . . c6 after white opens with 1. e4. After gaining popularity in the 1900s, it is now the fourth most popular move for black after 1. e4, following 1 . . . c5 (the Sicilian Defense, page 54), 1 . . . e5, and 1 . . . e6 (the French Defense, page 48).

■ CARO-KANN DEFENSE MOVES ■

1. e4	c6
2. d4	d5

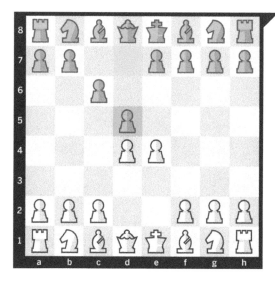

With their first move, black creates a mini pawn chain and prepares to attack the center. On the second move, black blockades white's d4 pawn and offers a trade with 2 . . . d5.

Now white can choose the Main Line with 3. Nc3 or the Advance Variation with 3. e5.

Main Line

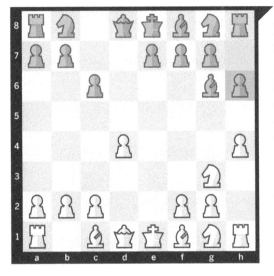

If white plays 3. Nc3, black usually plays 3 . . . dxe4. White then captures back with the knight: 4. Nxe4, and black plays 4 . . . Bf5, known as the Classical Variation. This move develops the bishop and hits white's knight. The knight must then run away with 5. Ng3, attacking black's bishop, which also retreats with 5 . . . Bg6. Now white plays the surprising move 6. h4, preparing to trap black's bishop with h5. Black must play 6 . . . h6 to give the bishop a place to hide.

Variation: Advance

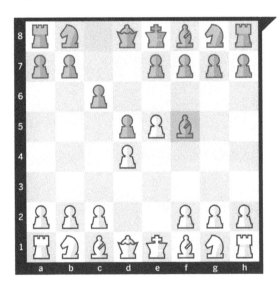

If white plays 3. e5 instead, they get the space advantage, but the center is closed. This position therefore lends itself to strategic, rather than tactical, play. It's important for black to bring the bishop out with 3 . . . Bf5, before closing it in forever with a move like . . . e6.

Plans for white: In the Classical Variation, it's important to trade off the light-squared bishop, so after h4, Nf3, h5, white will play Bd3, forcing the trade. Black will take and white takes back with the queen and ultimately castles queenside. In the Advance Variation, white will castle kingside and play continues on either side of the board.

Plans for black: In the Classical Variation, black will eventually have to play . . . Bh7 after it's kicked back by a pawn. The queenside knight will come to d7 since the pawn blocks it from going to c6. Black will play . . . e6 and . . . Be7 and castle kingside with a solid structure. In the Advance Variation, black develops all their pieces before castling. The knights must come to d7 and e7.

SICILIAN DEFENSE

The Sicilian is the most aggressive tactical defense for black. It avoids countless opening traps that can happen after white plays 1. e4 by playing 1 . . . c5, which attacks the center from the side. There are tons of variations in the Sicilian Defense; for now, let's concentrate on the main ideas behind . . . c5, and how best to get your pieces developed so you can castle.

The open Sicilians are called such because at some point white will play d4. Usually, they will bring their knight to f3 to guard d4 first. But whenever that pawn comes to d4, you take it with your pawn that's on c5. Black has achieved capturing a center pawn, so they still have both, whereas white has only the e-pawn. There are closed Sicilians as well, but they are less common.

■ **OPEN SICILIAN MOVES** ■

1. e4	c5
2. Nf3	d6 (pawn chain!)
3. d4	cd

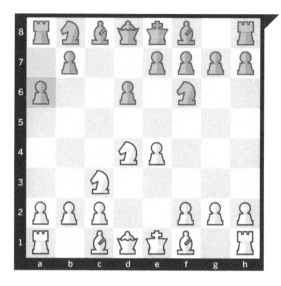

Now both sides continue to develop with 4. Nxd4 and 4 . . . Nf6, which attacks e4. After white plays 5. Nc3 to guard e4, black has choices. Try 5 . . . a6 (the Najdorf Variation), which prevents three pieces from annoying you on b5, and prepares . . . b5 at some point.

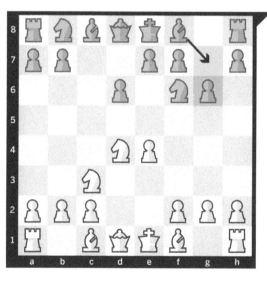

You can also simply play 5 . . . Nc6 in the Classical Variation. Or try 5 . . . g6 (the Dragon Variation) to fianchetto your bishop on the long diagonal. The Dragon is played much less frequently at the top levels these days, but it's extremely instructive for how to attack quickly.

White opts to castle queenside in many of these variations. Opponents castling on opposite sides means that whoever is the faster attacker wins.

Plans for white: In the Open Sicilian, after the center pawn has been traded, your long-range pieces become more dangerous. White will develop the queenside pieces with moves such as Be3 and Qd2 (creating a battery that aims at black's kingside), castle queenside, then pawn storm with moves such as f3, g4, and g5.

Plans for black: This is a tactical opening, so look for tricks. In the sharp Najdorf Variation, after white develops the bishop to e3, black will play . . . e5, kicking white's knight on d4, which must retreat to b3. The bishops will come to e6 and e7, and eventually black will pawn storm starting with . . . b5, . . . b4, and even . . . a5. Black will have many attacking opportunities by ignoring white's threats, when possible, with counterattacks on the queenside, where white is castled.

PETROV'S DEFENSE

Sometimes called the Russian Defense, this response to white's 1. e4 can go terribly wrong if you don't know the correct move order. Named after Alexander Petrov, this defense became popular in the mid-19th century.

■ **PETROV'S DEFENSE MOVES** ■

1. e4	e5
2. Nf3	Nf6

This symmetry is the start of the Petrov. It's crucial not to continue to copy your opponent, however! After the Classical Variation, where white simply captures on e5, black may not safely capture on e4, due to the open line to the king, and the fact that when you're copying, you're going second—any checks will prevent you from continuing your copying journey.

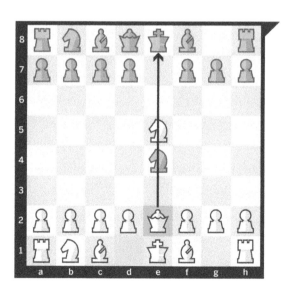

Watch what happens if black takes the pawn now. White plays 4. Qe2, lining up with the king.

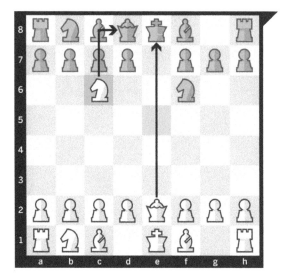

Clearly, there are already issues. If black continues to copy with 4 . . . Qe7, white simply snatches up the knight. (Black won't want to copy that move because their queen will hang.) If instead the knight runs back to f6, there is only one knight between white's queen and black's king. Do you see the discovered check?

That's right, 5. Nc6+. This devastating move wins black's queen. Notice that nothing can capture the knight on c6 because of the check by white's queen, which must be dealt with first. And if the black queen blocks, you'll still play knight takes queen.

Instead, after 3. Nxe5, black immediately plays 3 . . . d6, which kicks the knight back: 4. Nf3. Now black can capture the e4-pawn safely: 4 . . . Nxe4. In the Classical Attack, white now pushes 5. d4 and black responds with 5 . . . d5. Both sides will castle kingside.

Plans for white: White generally continues to develop with Bd3 and castles on the kingside. They will look for a kingside attack after developing the queenside pieces.

Plans for black: Because of the symmetrical pawn structure, there are no strategic imbalances, so black often has good drawing chances. As more pieces trade off, the more likely a draw will become.

SCANDINAVIAN DEFENSE

Although definitively the oldest opening recorded in chess, the Scandinavian (formerly known as the Center Counter Defense) has never really become mainstream. This is perhaps because it breaks one of the standard opening principles: Don't develop your queen early (or else she'll get kicked around by other pieces). Nevertheless, it features early open lines, allowing for the long-range pieces to start attacking. It is defined by black's brazen response to 1. e4: . . . d5. White must capture immediately, and typically black takes the pawn back with the queen.

■ **SCANDINAVIAN DEFENSE MOVES** ■

1. e4	d5
2. ed	Qxd5

Main Line (Mieses-Kotrč)

In this variation, white kicks black's queen away immediately with 3. Nc3. This move also develops a piece and gains a tempo.

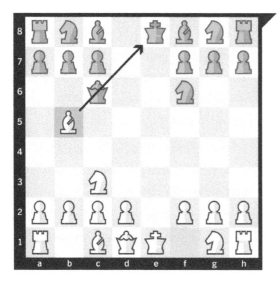

Black's queen has a few choices, but typically retreats with 3 . . . Qa5. Be careful not to retreat the queen to c6, where black would lose immediately to white's 4. Bb5, pinning and winning the queen!

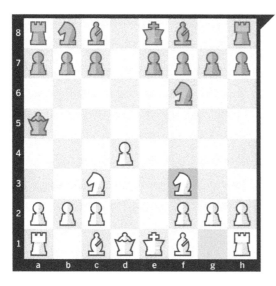

Instead, both sides continue to develop normally with 4. d4 Nf6, and 5. Nf3.

Black will now create a solid pawn structure in the center starting with 5 . . . c6. This gives the queen a chance to come back to c7, and also fights for control of d5. White generally scores well out of this opening.

Plans for white: White's pieces will develop naturally. Bc4, Bd2, and Qe2 are strong moves, and white also can castle on either side. The setup is solid for both sides, with white enjoying more space. If black plays . . . Bb4, white can play a3 to ask its intentions, and continue expanding on the queenside (if white has castled kingside).

Plans for black: Get the light-squared bishop out before pushing the e-pawn to e6, which lets out the dark-squared bishop. Your bishops will be your main attacking pieces in an open game. After the knight comes from b8 to d7, black will be able to castle on either side of the board.

PIRC DEFENSE

The Pirc (pronounced "peerts") is a hypermodern opening for black, meaning no immediate control of the center is taken with a pawn. The Yugoslavian (now Slovenian) GM Vasja Pirc was a proponent of this opening in the 1950s and '60s. Because it is relatively new, there is less theory, and although it was common in the 1970s, it has fallen out of fashion again at the highest levels. The Pirc is defined by the response to white's 1. e4 with 1 . . . d6.

Main Line

The idea for black in this defense is to attack the center from the side with their fianchetto bishop while also preparing to play either . . . e5 or . . . c5 at some point to strike at the center. Pushing the pawn to . . . d6 prepares both moves.

■ PIRC DEFENSE MOVES ■

1. e4	d6
2. d4	Nf6
3. Nc3	g6

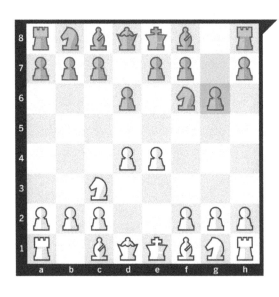

White has two equally popular choices on move 4: the aggressive Austrian Attack with 4. f4, or the Classical Variation with 4. Nf3.

Variation: Austrian Attack

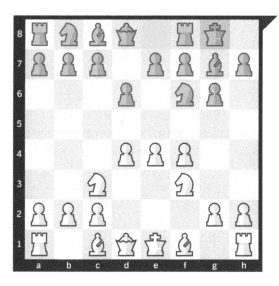

After 4. f4 Bg7 and 5. Nf3 0-0, white has a huge pawn wall in the center, but black is already castled. This game will be a fight for the center.

Variation: Classical

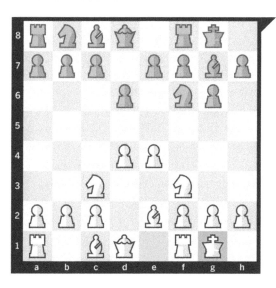

The Classical Variation is a little quieter (white's fifth move is literally called the Quiet System), but still easy to play for white: 4. Nf3 Bg7, 5. Be2, and both sides castle kingside.

Plans for white: Once trades happen in the center, white's pieces will have more scope. If black plays . . . e5, it will shut in their own fianchetto bishop. White continues to develop their pieces to natural squares and can attack on any side of the board in the middle game. There is a lot of flexibility.

Plans for black: Black will need to strike in the center at some point. In the Austrian Attack, black continues to develop and waits for white to play e5 when they will trade in the center. And in the Classical, black will play . . . c6, . . . Nbd7, and eventually push . . . e5 themself.

MODERN DEFENSE

Closely related to the Pirc Defense (page 62) is the Modern, which is also a hypermodern opening. This defense for black after 1. e4 continues with 1 . . . g6, immediately fianchettoing the bishop to g7. Because black does not take the center with a pawn, white must.

There is less theory to memorize in this opening and its variations. It is a more positional game, however, so black must strike at the center at some point. As in the Pirc Defense, black delays playing . . . Nf6. There are pros and cons to every move, and although this move makes the fianchetto bishop stronger, and moves such as e5 by white don't attack a knight on f6, it also delays black's castling.

■ MODERN DEFENSE MOVES ■

1. e4	g6
2. d4	Bg7

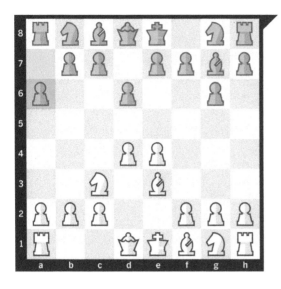

In the Standard Line, white plays 3. Nc3 and black plays 3 . . . d6, a preparatory pawn move that will allow for a later strike in the center. White continues to develop with 4. Be3 while black plays 4 . . . a6 to prepare to claim b5 for themself.

After 5. Qd2 b5, white is ready to castle queenside, although it continues to delay in favor of strengthening the center by pushing to f3 and further piece development.

Plans for white: White can opt for an early kingside attack with moves such as h4, which black will need to immediately stop with . . . h5. If not, white can create a crushing pawn storm on the kingside with g4 and eventually h5. Notice white already has a queen and bishop battery aiming at the kingside. White castles long (queenside) and develops their pieces to the best squares, so white will be in the best position to recapture when black finally attacks the center.

Plans for black: This is a flexible opening, and black's counterattacks can be very strong. Black can delay castling because there is no tension in the center, and no pawn trades creating open lines to the king. Black must be careful not to move too many pawns though, as there are already a lot of pawn moves in this opening. Moving a pawn means you aren't developing a back-rank piece, which goes against our principles of "center, develop, castle." Develop the knight from b8 to d7 and fianchetto the light-squared bishop. When white castles queenside, black can play . . . c5 and then . . . Qa5 for a queenside attack.

QUEEN'S GAMBIT

This is the oldest chess opening still played today. It was first mentioned in a manuscript in 1490 but didn't gain popularity until centuries later, when positional play was given more credence.

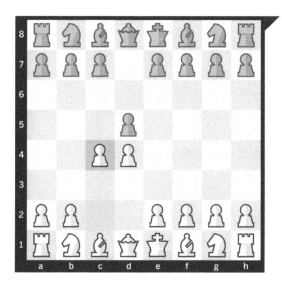

White starts by attacking the center with their queen's pawn, 1. d4. This prevents both 1 . . . e5 and the Sicilian 1 . . . c5 because you could just take those pawns. Black can play 1 . . . d5 or 1 . . . Nf6. In either case, you'll play 2. c4, which creates a pawn wall.

This opening is called a *gambit* because your c-pawn appears to be hanging, but if black takes it with 2 . . . dxc4, known as the Queen's Gambit Accepted, you'll be able to easily win it back with either 3. e3 or 3. e4 and a discovered attack on c4 by your bishop on f1, or the immediate 3. Qa4+, a double attack on the king and pawn on c4.

White controls the center.

In either case, white has achieved pulling black's pawn away from the center while still maintaining their own two center pawns.

More common at the higher levels is to see black play 2 . . . e6, the Queen's Gambit Declined or 2 . . . c6 (the Slav Defense, page 70). After black plays 2 . . . e6, white develops the knight behind the c-pawn with 3. Nc3. Black can play the most common move 3 . . . Nf6 to attack the center and prepare to castle. Notice that both players are maintaining tension in the center.

■ **QUEEN'S GAMBIT DECLINED MOVES** ■

1. d4	d5
2. c4	e6
3. Nc3	Nf6

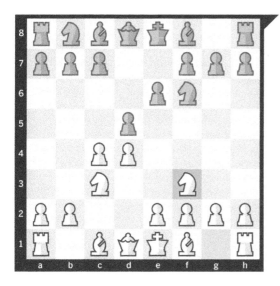

White has many options to continue development. A common one, 4. Nf3, also known as the Queen's Gambit Declined: Three Knights Variation, looks like the diagram to the left.

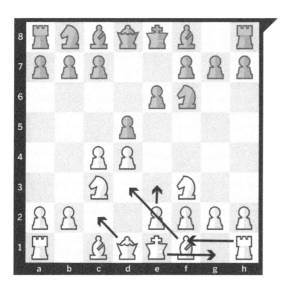

Plans for white: In any queen's pawn opening, it's important to bring your c-pawn out before developing the knight to c3. Otherwise, your position will be cramped. In the Queen's Gambit Declined (QGD): Three Knights Variation, next white will play moves such as e3, Qc2, Bd3, and 0-0 with a kingside attack.

Plans for black: You can capture on c4 after white has played Bd3. Then white must waste a tempo using their bishop to capture back. Black can play 4 . . . Be7 and then castle in the Three Knights Variation. If continuing in the Semi-Slav Defense (page 72), black will play 4 . . . c6 to solidify the center, . . . Nbd7, . . . Bd6, and castles (kingside).

SLAV DEFENSE

Although this response to the Queen's Gambit (page 67) was first seen in 1590, it did not become fully analyzed until the 1920s and '30s, mainly by the Russian player Semyon Alapin. The Slav is the most popular response after 1. d4 d5 and 2. c4, which offers the c-pawn and attacks black's center pawn from the side. Black solidifies with 2 . . . c6 to avoid blocking in the light-squared bishop (note that this does take away the natural square for the b8-knight).

■ SLAV DEFENSE MOVES ■

1. d4	d5
2. c4	c6

The most common contemporary move is the Modern Line, with 3. Nf3, when black responds with 3 . . . Nf6.

From here, both sides will continue to develop as normal. Often after 4. Nc3, black will choose to transpose into the Semi-Slav Defense (page 72) with 4 . . . e6.

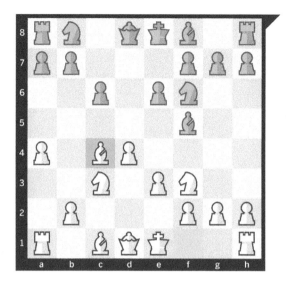

If instead black continues in the Main Line (also called the Modern, Alapin Variation, Czech, Classical System), after 4. Nc3 black will now take on c4: 4 . . . cxd4. White plays 5. a4, which prevents black from trying to hold on to the c-pawn by playing . . . b5. Black plays 5 . . . Bf5, getting the bishop out before pushing the e-pawn, which would lock the bishop inside the pawn chain. White plays 6. e3, a discovered attack on the c-pawn, and black plays 6 . . . e6 to let the dark-squared bishop out. Finally, white will capture: 7. Bxc4.

Plans for white: White castles soon on the kingside and will try to create a strong center by pushing e4. This move also allows the dark-squared bishop to develop. Another idea is Nf3-h4, attacking the bishop on f5 and often forcing the trade of knight for bishop.

Plans for black: Typically, black develops the dark-squared bishop to b4 and castles kingside next. White will get a strong center, but if they overextend, black can break through to white's king.

SEMI-SLAV DEFENSE

Though the Semi-Slav, like the Slav Defense (page 70), arises from the Queen's Gambit (page 67), its popularity, heavy theory, and attacking games have earned it a title as its own opening, not just a variation.

■ **SEMI-SLAV DEFENSE MOVES** ■

1. d4	d5
2. c4	c6
3. Nf3	Nf6
4. Nc3	e6

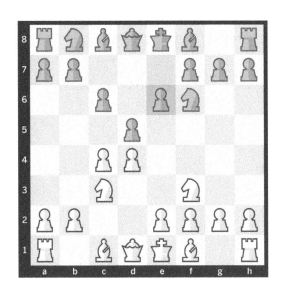

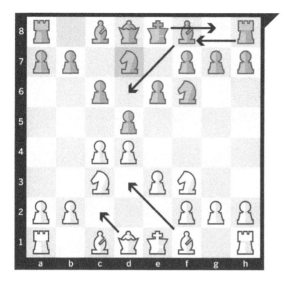

Notice that black blocks in their light-squared bishop on c8 for a while. After the Main Line, 5. e3 and 5 . . . Nbd7, both sides will quickly develop and castle kingside.

Plans for white: White's moves should feel natural. The queen goes to c2 and the bishop goes to d3, creating a battery that directly aims at black's castled king. White will need to try for a pawn push to e4 to let out the dark-squared bishop.

Plans for black: Black will need to cover some of the dark squares that became weak when they placed all their center pawns on white squares. The way to do that is by playing . . . Bd6. When white develops their light-squared bishop, black can finally capture on c4, making white lose a tempo with the bishop by capturing it back. After castling, the light-squared bishop can be fianchettoed on b7. Black's pieces will develop on the queenside and aim at the kingside.

TARRASCH DEFENSE

The Tarrasch was developed by German theoretician Siegbert Tarrasch. You may remember the Tarrasch Variation in the French Defense (page 48). In the Tarrasch Defense specifically, 1. d4 d5 is played on the first move, whereas the aggressive . . . c5 occurs on move 3.

■ TARRASCH DEFENSE MOVES ■

1. d4	d5
2. c4	e6
3. Nc3	c5

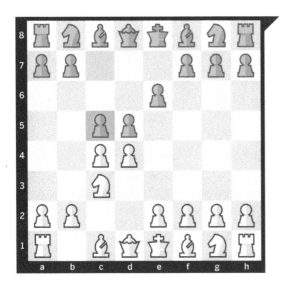

The idea behind these Main Line moves is for black to attack the center and provoke pawn trades.

Main Line: Two Knights Variation

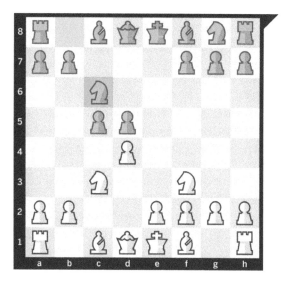

White now typically captures toward the center with 4. cxd5 and black takes back with 4 . . . exd5. Both sides continue by developing their knights: 5. Nf3 and 5 . . . Nc6.

Variation: Two Knights, Rubinstein System

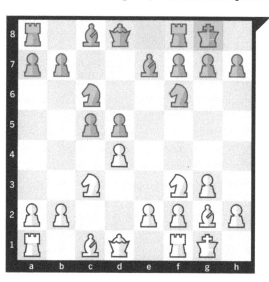

To fianchetto and castle, white plays 6. g3. Black continues with 6 . . . Nf6, and now everyone develops their bishops: 7. Bg2 Be7, and finally 8. 0-0 0-0.

Note that sometimes white may play 3. Nf3 instead of 3. Nc3. This is technically considered a variation of the Queen's Gambit Declined (page 68), and after black plays 3 . . . c5, it is called the Pseudo-Tarrasch or Semi-Tarrasch Defense. Sometimes it will transpose into a straight Tarrasch later in the opening.

Plans for white: After developing the dark-squared bishop and waiting for black to trade the c-pawn for the d-pawn, white will blockade black's isolated d-pawn with a knight. Then white will enjoy the open files by placing the rook on c1 at some point and utilizing their two bishops in an attack.

Plans for black: Black would like to hold on to the d-pawn and even push it but can't always. Black might go for a kingside attack, considering white has already pushed a pawn to g3, which can lead to a weakness on the light squares.

GRÜNFELD DEFENSE

This active opening named after 1920s GM Ernst Grünfeld features a similar but safe line for black after 1. d4, where black prepares to fianchetto the bishop. Although it has been played in top level chess, it is not especially popular these days. Nevertheless, it is a fun and useful opening for black to play against 1. d4. Instead of allowing white a massive center, black strikes at the center with the important move . . . d5 on move 3.

■ GRÜNFELD DEFENSE MOVES ■

1. d4	Nf6
2. c4	g6
3. Nc3	d5

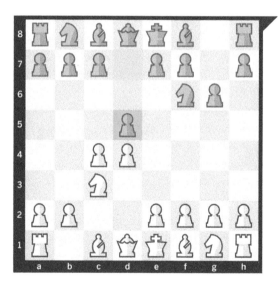

Note how white has a pawn wall in the center, and black is both getting ready to castle and counter-attacking the center before fianchettoing the dark-squared bishop.

Variation: Exchange

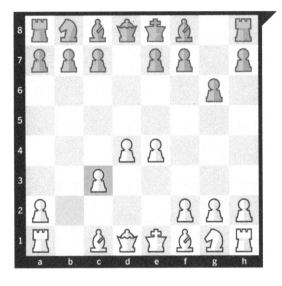

The most common variation played is the Exchange Variation, where white captures the d-pawn that's just been pushed: 4. cd. Black must take back with the knight: 4 . . . Nxd5. Now white can create a new pawn wall with 5. e4, attacking the knight. Black captures white's knight on c3, and white takes back: 5 . . . Nxc3 6. bxc3.

White's center is super strong right now, but not infallible. Black will continue to focus their attack to destroy it, developing their pieces to natural squares, and aiming directly at d4. Note that it's worth sacrificing a pawn just to break up the center.

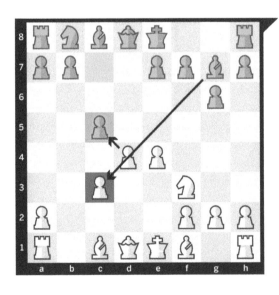

After black plays 6 . . . Bg7 and white develops 7. Nf3, the critical move to remember for black is 7 . . . c5, which directly counterattacks the center. Notice that white can't take the pawn immediately, because of the pin on c3.

Plans for white: Try the move 8. Rb1 (Modern Exchange Variation), where white grabs the open file. Next, the light-squared bishop is brought to e2, and white will push the pawn to d5, avoiding the pawn trade and all the pressure on d4. Don't forget to castle!

Plans for black: Black will continue to mount pressure on d4. Already the fianchettoed bishop, the pawn on c5, and the queen attack d4. Next, black will castle and play . . . Nc6 to attack d4 again. And a move such as . . . Bg4 will attack one of white's defenders of d4. This fight is all about the center.

LONDON SYSTEM

This opening for white gained popularity after the 1922 London Congress Tournament. It is defined by white's moves 1. d4 and 2. Nf3 followed by Bf4 or an immediate 2. Bf4 (considered theoretically slightly better), and is currently a favorite of World Champion Magnus Carlsen. It is called a *system* because it can be played against pretty much anything black tries, making it a remarkably versatile opening.

There is significant flexibility in the move order for this system, and less theory than in other openings. Black can play 1 . . . Nf6 then 2 . . . d5, or first, 1 . . . d5 and 2 . . . Nf6, preparing to fianchetto the bishop on g7. This is an "Indian Game" setup, which refers to any game in which black plays . . . Nf6 in response to d4. Here, white aims to create a solid pawn structure with the moves e3 and c3.

Main Line

1. d4	Nf6
2. Nf3	d5
3. Bf4	c5
4. e3	Nc6
5. c3	e6

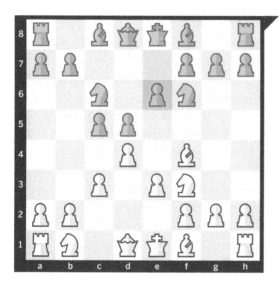

Note that no pawns have been captured yet, making this a closed center, and castling can be delayed in games where the center is closed.

White continues development with 6. Nbd2, since it can't go to c3, and from here it nicely controls c4 and e4. Now black develops the bishop offering a trade with 6 . . . Bd6. It is not beneficial for white to take black's bishop on d6, because that would help black develop their queen when they capture back.

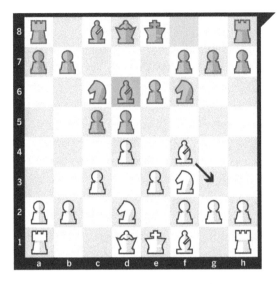

Therefore, on move 7, white retreats the bishop to g3 to preserve their pawn structure (if the bishop gets captured, white won't have to capture away from the center). If black then takes on g3, white can happily capture back with the h-pawn, which opens the rook's file for attacks on black's king once they castle.

Plans for white: White will play Bd3 next, nicely covering the white squares since their pawns are on dark squares in the center. White will continue to press in the center with Ne5 and f4, guarding the knight again. Eventually, white castles kingside and attacks black's kingside.

Plans for black: After castling, black continues to develop the queen-side bishop by fianchettoing it. Both sides maintain the tension in the center for as long as possible. Black will attack either the center or the queenside.

NIMZO-INDIAN DEFENSE

There are many Indian Defenses, first developed by the Bengali player Moheschunder Bannerjee in the 1800s; they are classified as any 1. d4 Nf6 responses by black. The Latvia-born Danish chess player and writer Aron Nimzowitsch popularized the following continuation, which attacks the center from the side. This positionally sound defense is a solid way for black to respond to the queen's pawn coming out first.

■ NIMZO-INDIAN DEFENSE MOVES ■

1. d4	Nf6
2. c4	e6
3. Nc3	Bb4

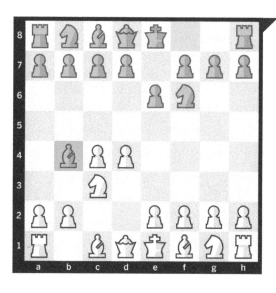

White has many options for their fourth move, but in general will have a stronger center than black. However, black's pin can be annoying. The most common variation, called either the Normal Line or the Rubinstein Variation, is 4. e3.

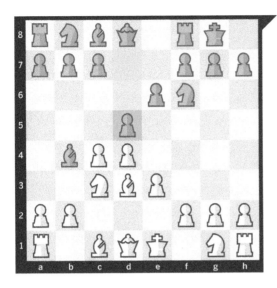

Whether white plays 4. e3 or 4. Qc2 (the Classical Variation), black will castle on move four. Most common for white now is to develop the bishop to d3 where it attacks black's kingside. Notice black hasn't put a pawn in the center yet; now is the time! 5 . . . d5.

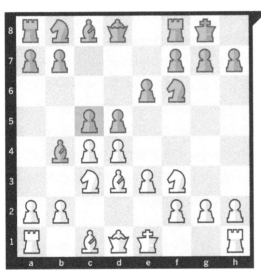

White maintains the tension in the center and plays 6. Nf3 preparing to castle. Black adds more pressure to the center with 6 . . . c5. Notice black has yet to take on c3! They are waiting for a3, then black will capture the knight.

Plans for white: If you don't want to have your pawns doubled on the c-file, you can play Qc2, the Classical Variation, and capture back on c3 with your queen. If you don't mind the doubled pawns, continue to develop as normal, and try to open the position, as you'll have two bishops.

Plans for black: The compensation for trading a bishop for knight is that white will have doubled pawns. This pawn structure will be a long-term weakness for white. If you trade your bishop for the knight on c3, be sure to keep the position closed (no pawn trades) to benefit your two knights.

KING'S INDIAN DEFENSE

Another sharp opening is the King's Indian Defense (KID). Although it has been around for centuries, most Masters considered it dubious because it allowed white too much control over the center. It only became popular in the 1920s with the rise of hypermodernism. In it, black allows white to set up a strong center, then aims to counterattack the center later. This opening is less common at the top levels, but it's exciting and often leads to a decisive result.

■ **KING'S INDIAN DEFENSE MOVES (NORMAL VARIATION)** ■

1. d4	Nf6
2. c4	g6
3. Nc3	Bg7
4. e4	d6
5. Nf3	0-0

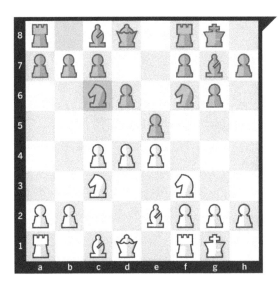

Typically, white continues with 6. Be2 (the Orthodox Variation) and black plays 6 . . . e5, then white castles 7. 0-0 and 7 . . . Nc6 (the Orthodox Aronin-Taimanov Defense).

White is allowed three pawns in the center before black counters the center with . . . e5. But black has also fianchettoed the dark-squared bishop and castled early. Black will go for a kingside checkmating attack, whereas white generally aims at the queenside.

Sämisch Variation

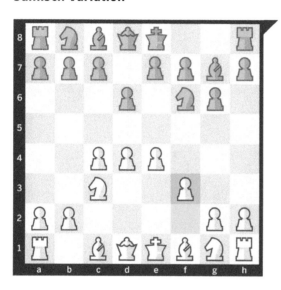

A popular variation of the KID is the Sämisch, in which white plays 5. f3 to solidify the center and prevent black's knight from landing on g4.

Players generally castle on opposite sides, meaning that whoever is the faster attacker wins.

Plans for white: After taking immediate control of the center with pawns, in the Sämisch, white's plans are similar to those when playing against the Sicilian: f3, Be3, Qd2, and 0-0-0. White generally keeps the center closed by pushing to d5, as this locks black's bishop in on g7 (since the e-pawns are frozen).

Plans for black: Be prepared to counterattack. Try for a kingside attack with . . . Nh5 and . . . f5, striking at the center and opening black's rook up to help with the attack. Remember that knights become very important pieces in closed positions, because they are the only ones that can jump.

BENONI DEFENSE

The name Ben-oni is Hebrew for "son of my sorrow," and it is part of the title of a chess book by Aaron Reinganum (in English, *Son of Sorrow, or Defenses Against Gambits in Chess*) published in 1825, where this opening is first discussed.

■ BENONI DEFENSE MOVES ■

1. d4	Nf6
2. c4	c5

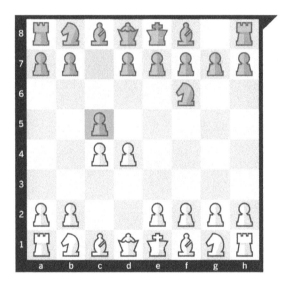

After 2. c4, black typically plays . . . e6 (which can lead to the Queen's Gambit Declined or the Nimzo-Indian Defense, pages 68 and 83), . . . g6 (King's Indian Defense, page 86), or . . . c5.

In this section, let's explore 2 . . . c5. This move means an early attack in the center. And although it appears the c-pawn is hanging, remember that often these pawns are "gambited" because the compensation is worth it: Pulling your opponent's pawn away from the center is enough. In play, this pawn is almost never captured, and instead white opts for 3. d5.

Variation: Benko Gambit

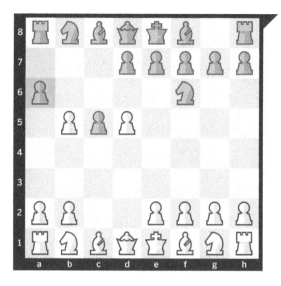

In response, black may enter the Benko Gambit with 3 . . . b5, choosing to sacrifice pawns for long-term positional compensation. White will accept this gambit by playing 4. cxb5 and now black plays 4 . . . a6, offering another pawn which is eventually traded. Black's strategy is to open lines for development.

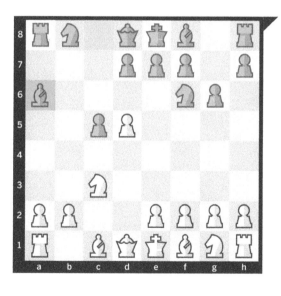

White captures this pawn, too, with 5. bxa6, and although black can take it back immediately, more often black uses this moment to play 5 . . . g6, in order to fianchetto. After 6. Nc3 Bxa6, you have the Benko Gambit: Fully Accepted.

Plans for white: It is preferred to decline the first sacrifice and not allow black all the open lines. Surprisingly, although it is more common for white to take on b5, white scores higher by declining with 3. Nf3 (Benko Gambit Declined: Main Line). If accepting the gambit, white should try to fianchetto their own light-squared bishop in what's called Fully Accepted: Fianchetto Attack.

Plans for black: Black will fianchetto and castle kingside. The knight from b8 goes to d7, and if white plays e4, black will snatch up the bishop on f1 with the bishop on a6. That prevents white from castling since they must take back with the king.

ENGLISH OPENING

This opening gets its name from Howard Staunton, the famous 19th-century English Master who also promoted the standardized chess pieces still used today. The English was most popular from the 1960s to the 1980s but is still used today. It is considered a hypermodern and positional opening, rather than a tactical one.

The defining move of the English is 1. c4.

Black has many options to respond. They can play 1 . . . Nf6, where white should now push 2. d4 since black has not put a pawn in the center (another Indian Game). Black can also attack the center with 1 . . . e5, where white generally responds with 2. Nc3 in a Reversed Sicilian Variation. Or black might try 1 . . . c5, the Symmetrical English.

Variation: Four Knights

After the first move, the most common strategy for both white and black is to develop their knights to the center in the Four Knights Variation.

■ **ENGLISH OPENING MOVES** ■

1. c4	e5
2. Nc3	Nf6
3. Nf3	Nc6

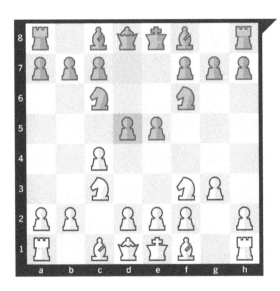

White typically plays 4. g3 to fianchetto the bishop to g2 and castle kingside. Black can play 4 . . . d5 and, just as in the Sicilian Defense (page 54), when that d-pawn comes out, the c-pawn is ready to take it.

Plans for white: Traditionally in the English, white will fianchetto and castle kingside. There will be a fight for the center, and white will play on the queenside in the middle game, with the b-pawn sometimes becoming a dangerous passed pawn in the endgame.

Plans for black: Set up your pawns in a way that is most comfortable for you to develop your pieces. If you are used to immediately attacking the center, go for 1 . . . e5. Your pieces will go to typical squares, and generally black will prepare a kingside attack.

RÉTI OPENING

This opening was developed by Richard Réti, an Austro-Hungarian player for the Czech Republic. It opens with 1. Nf3, allowing black many responses. This flexible first move by white can transpose into several other openings, such as the English Opening (page 91), Queen's Gambit (page 67), King's Indian Defense (page 86), or Sicilian Defense (page 54). It's a very popular opening, and white sometimes will employ this first to see which opening black chooses.

Black can play 1 . . . Nf6 and similarly wait to see if white will strike the center with 2. d4 or 2. c4. White's push to d4 could lead to a Queen's Gambit (page 67), created with the move 3. c4 which creates a pawn wall with the d-pawn (Queen's Gambit Declined, page 68, with . . . e6, or Slav Defense, page 70, with . . . c6). If white plays 2. c4, the game will look like the English Opening (page 91).

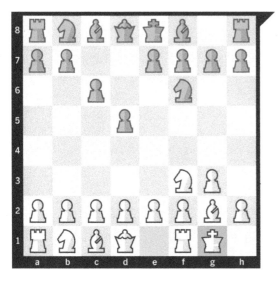

White might also play 2. g3, known as the King's Indian Attack, where white immediately fianchettoes and castles. This system can be played against almost any moves by black.

Another first move by black could be 1 . . . d5, which immediately attacks the center. White again has the choice of the King's Indian Attack with 2. g3, or 2. d4, which transforms the game into a queen's pawn opening.

Plans for white: Try to make a pawn wall with c4 and d4. You should be comfortable playing a Queen's Gambit and an English. The light-squared bishop can be fianchettoed or developed after e3. Do not play both g3 and e3, because this weakens the light squares; the bishop can defend/attack only one of those diagonals that you've opened. Play will occur in the center and queenside.

Plans for black: Choose the opening you're most comfortable with. If you like the King's Indian Defense (page 86) setup, you can fianchetto; if you like the solid center, you can go for a Slav Defense (page 70) or Semi-Slav Defense (page 72). If white plays c4 after you've played . . . d5, do not accept this "gambit" pawn, as it draws away your center pawn toward the side, and you can't hold on to it anyway. This is a positional opening, so always try to get your pieces to their most active squares.

CATALAN OPENING

A more strategic, rather than tactical, opening is the Catalan. This opening gets its name from a 1929 tournament in Barcelona, where GM Savielly Tartakower developed the system. The opening can transpose into an Indian Game if black fianchettoes, or an English Opening (page 91). But the main moves are as follows.

■ **CATALAN OPENING MOVES** ■

1. d4	Nf6
2. c4	e6
3. g3	d5
4. Nf3	

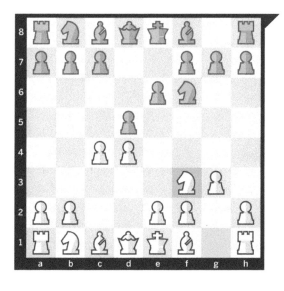

After white develops this knight, black can choose to play 4 . . . Be7 and 5 . . . 0-0, and then capture the pawn on c4, or 4 . . . dc immediately. In both cases, white calmly fianchettoes the bishop on move 5.

When black challenges the center with 3 . . . d5, tension develops between the c- and d-pawns. Note how white leaves the c-pawn and focuses instead on development with 4. Nf3.

Black has the option of capturing the c-pawn in the Open Catalan (more popular) or reinforcing the d-pawn, in a Closed Catalan.

Variation: Open

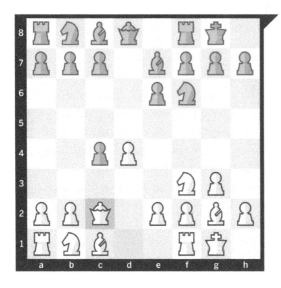

In the Open Defense, Classical Line, black will take the pawn on c4. This opens white's fianchettoed bishop, and sometimes black will try to trade light-squared bishops to neutralize the opposing bishop's power. Most of the time, black cannot hold on to their pawn. White can play Qc2 or Qa4, and trying to keep the pawn will be challenging for black.

Variation: Closed

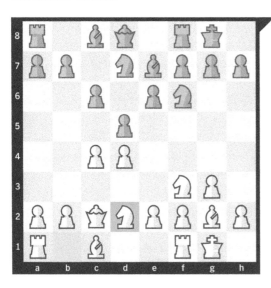

In the Closed Catalan, after both sides castle, black plays 6 . . . c6. After 7. Qc2, both players develop their knights to d7 and d2, and black will fianchetto the light-squared bishop. Because black's pawns are on light squares, the bishop does not have much attacking range for the moment.

Plans for white: Usually white will go for a center or queenside attack because of the kingside fianchettoed bishop. If black has kept the position closed, white will need to play e4 and e5 to gain space in the center. Positional openings require you to get your pieces to the best squares and create a favorable pawn structure.

Plans for black: In the Open Catalan, black will need to find a way to blunt the light-squared bishop, maybe by bringing their bishop from c8-d7-c6 or in the Closed Catalan, to fianchetto their light-squared bishop. If you take on c4, don't worry about holding on to your pawn. Continue to develop your queenside pieces. Because of all the tension in this opening, it is not for the faint of heart.

PART III

Strategy Challenges

It's time to test your understanding of the openings to see what you've learned. Here are twenty challenges that ask for specific moves. Use the answer key at the back of the book to check your work. If you get the answer wrong, be sure to go back to that opening and review. Remember that setting up the diagrams on a physical chessboard will help with muscle memory of the right moves, too. Good luck!

(Answers on page 113.)

1. The Italian Game

You have completed the first three moves of the Italian, and black has just played 3 . . . Nf6. How would you continue to attack f7?

White to move:

(Answer on page 114.)

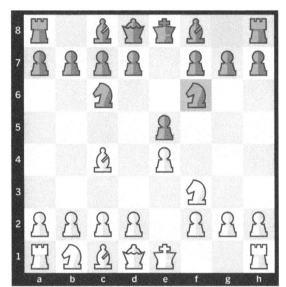

2. Ruy López

You have white in this position. Black has just played 3 . . . a6, attacking the bishop. Do you take the knight or retreat?

White to move:

(Answer on page 114.)

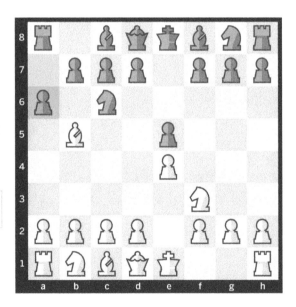

3. Sicilian Defense

You are playing black here. You'd like to continue with the most commonly played move, the Najdorf Variation. What move do you play? (Hint: It prepares to play . . . b5 at some point while also preventing three pieces from landing on b5.)
Black to move:

(Answer on page 115.)

4. Queen's Gambit

You have white. You'd like to play the Queen's Gambit; do you bring out your knight to c3 first, or move your pawn to c4 in this position?
White to move:

(Answer on page 115.)

5. Slav Defense

You're playing the Modern Line in the Slav as black, and white has just developed their knight to f3. You'd like to prepare to castle and also attack the center, but you aren't transposing to the Semi-Slav just yet. What move does black play to develop a piece on move 3?

Black to move:

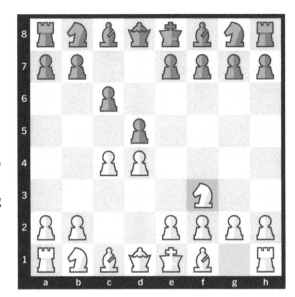

(Answer on page 116.)

6. Nimzo-Indian Defense

You are black in this position and aiming to play the Nimzo-Indian. What is the best move that pins a piece on move 3?

Black to move:

(Answer on page 116.)

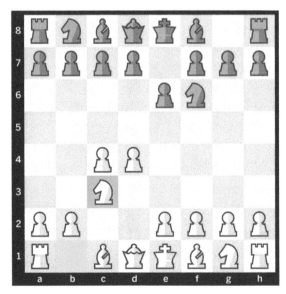

7. King's Indian Defense

You have black in the KID, and you know you need to strike at white's center. But there are two moves you must play first to prepare for the strike. What are they?

Black to move:

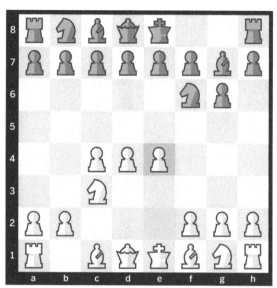

and [ ]

(Answer on page 117.)

8. French Defense

In this 1. e4 opening, black plays 1 . . . e6, the French. After 2. d4 d5 and 3. Nc3 Bb4, the Winawer Variation, white plays 4. e5, the Advance Variation in the Winawer. How must black strike at white's pawn chain: at the top with 4 . . . f6 or at the base with 4 . . . c5?

Black to move:

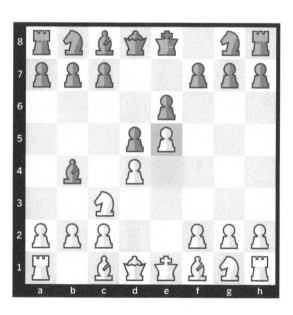

[ ]

(Answer on page 117.)

9. Grünfeld Defense

You're playing black in this 1. d4 opening and have reached the Exchange Variation of the Grünfeld. White has just created a new pawn wall with 5. e4, attacking your knight. Where do you move your knight?

Black to move:

(Answer on page 118.)

10. Catalan Opening

You have chosen to play the Catalan. After getting your pawn wall set up with 1. d4 Nf6 and 2. c4 e6, which move comes next? (Hint: Think about which way your bishop will develop.)

White to move:

(Answer on page 118.)

11. Petrov's Defense

Black is trying to play the Petrov but has made a terrible mistake. After 1. e4 e5, 2. Nf3 Nf6, and 3. Nxe5, black quickly captures the e-pawn back: 3 . . . Nxe4? How does white take advantage of the newly opened e-file that leads directly to black's king?

White to move:

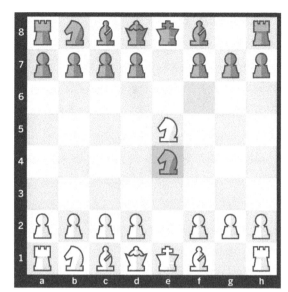

(Answer on page 119.)

12. English Opening

White is playing the English: Four Knights Variation. White was preparing to fianchetto and black has just played 4 . . . d5. What is the best move for white now?

White to move:

(Answer on page 119.)

13. Caro-Kann Defense

You're playing black and have responded to 1. e4 with the Caro-Kann: 1 . . . c6. After 2. d4 d5 white can play 3. Nc3 (Main Line) or 3. e5 (Advance). In both the Main Line: Classical Variation and the Advance Variation, which is the first back-rank piece to develop for black, and what square does it land on? (In the Classical it develops on move 4, and in the Advance it develops on move 3.)

Black to move:

(Answer on page 120.)

14. Scotch Opening

You'd like to attack the center right away in the Scotch. After you play 1. e4 e5 and 2. Nf3 Nc6, what move immediately challenges the center?

White to move:

(Answer on page 120.)

15. Fried Liver Attack

You have white in an Italian Game. After black stops your immediate capture of f7 by playing 4 ... d5, you take this pawn: 5. ed. Now black makes an egregious error: 5 ... Nxd5? What are the next two moves for white? (Hint: Remember "sac and attack!")

White to move:

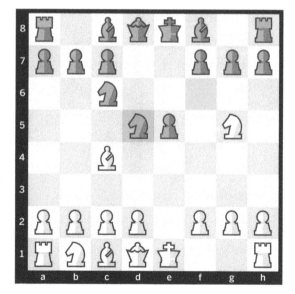

 **and**

(Answer on page 121.)

16. Scholar's Mate

You have black in this position. What is white's checkmate threat and how do you stop it?

White's checkmate threat:

[   ]

Black should play:

[   ]

(Answer on page 121.)

17. London System

In the London, what part of the opening is delayed because the center is closed? After white plays 1. d4, whether black plays 1 . . . Nf6 or 1 . . . d5, the London is defined by which move (it can occur on move 2 or 3)?

[   ]

is delayed. White to move:

[   ]

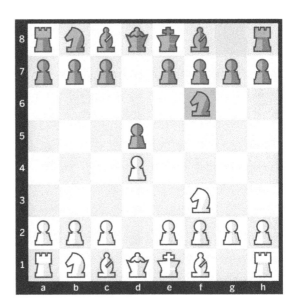

(Answer on page 122.)

18. Tarrasch Defense

You have black in this exciting opening with lots of attacks in the center. After 1. d4 d5 2. c4 e6 3. Nc3, how do you strike at the center again?

Black to move:

(Answer on page 122.)

19. Scandinavian Defense

You are playing black and go for the Scandinavian Defense after 1. e4. When you play 1 . . . d5, white captures 2. ed and you take back with your queen: 2 . . . Qxd5. In the Main Line, white will kick your queen with 3. Nc3. Where should she go?

Black to move:

(Answer on page 123.)

20. Pirc Defense

In this hypermodern opening, black delays attacking the center head-on, and instead attacks from the side and prepares to strike at the center later. After 1. e4 d6 2. d4 Nf6 3. Nc3, how does black proceed?

Black to move:

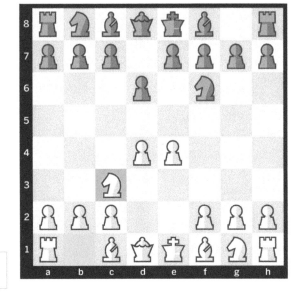

(Answer on page 123.)

Answer Key

1. The Italian Game, page 100

Answer: 4. Ng5 attacks f7 again. Now white is aiming at f7 with two pieces, and it's only defended once, by black's king. Black will have to play . . . d5 to block the bishop.

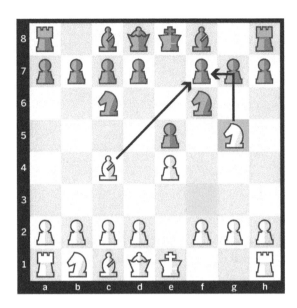

2. Ruy López, page 100

Answer: In the Morphy Defense Variation, you play 4. Ba4, retreating the bishop but still aiming at the knight. You don't want to capture the knight right away, thinking you're removing the guard of the e5 pawn, because black can recapture with their d-pawn and if you take Nxe5, black

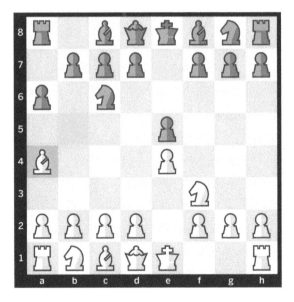

plays . . . Qd4, forking your knight and pawn, thereby winning the pawn back with a better position.

3. Sicilian Defense, page 101

Answer:
5 . . . a6 is the Najdorf and is currently the most popular and sharpest opening for black. This move stops Bb5+ and allows black to prepare to push to b5 themself at some point.

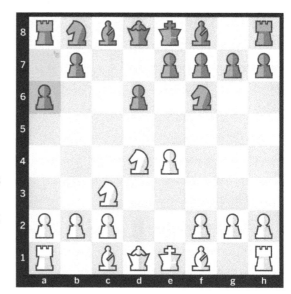

4. Queen's Gambit, page 101

Answer: Bring out the pawn first to c4, and then the knight afterward to c3.

5. Slav Defense, page 102

Answer: In the Modern Line, black will play 3 . . . Nf6. The Semi-Slav would be adding the move . . . e6 as well as . . . c6, which can still happen on black's next turn.

6. Nimzo-Indian Defense, page 102

Answer: Black plays the aggressive 3 . . . Bb4, which pins the knight on c3 and prepares to castle immediately!

7. King's Indian Defense, page 103

Answer: . . . d6 and . . . 0-0.

First, . . . d6 will take some control of the center and prepares to push . . . e5. Second, castling gets your king out of the center before it has the potential to open up with the pawn trade after you move to . . . e5.

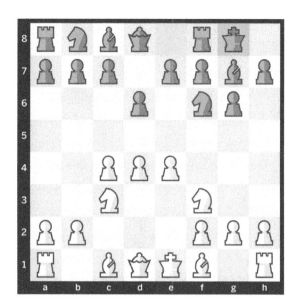

8. French Defense, page 103

Answer: Black must strike at the base of the pawn chain with 4 . . . c5! The base of the pawn chain is weakest because no pawns protect it. Also, it's dangerous to move your f-pawn, the weakest pawn at the start of the game: Notice that doing so opens the short diagonal to your king, which is hard to block checks on, and makes up the base of your pawn chain.

9. Grünfeld Defense, page 104

Answer: Capture the knight on c3. It is a wasted tempo to retreat, and doing so would give white a favorable position with an uncontested center. After the trade on c3, black will fianchetto the bishop and start to barrel down on d4.

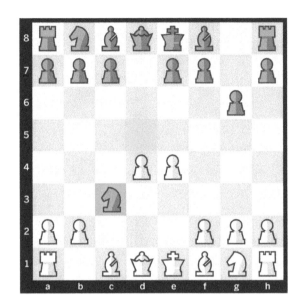

10. Catalan Opening, page 104

Answer: 3. g3 will prepare for white to fianchetto the bishop later. Black may challenge the center with 3 . . . d5 and white simply continues to develop with 4. Nf3, after which white will fianchetto and castle.

11. Petrov's Defense, page 105

Answer: 4. Qe2. The problem for black now is that the knight is under attack immediately and the king is open. So, if black plays 4 . . . Qe7, copying your queen move, you just take the knight, and they can't take your knight or else they lose their queen. More exciting, if their knight moves away, you have the delightful, discovered check Nc6+, winning the black queen, because your queen gives check.

12. English Opening, page 105

Answer: White must capture, 5. cxd5. The purpose of the opening is to attack the center from the side, and the purpose of 1. c4 is to aim at d5 with a pawn and snatch it up when black lands there. You can wait to fianchetto, but you can't wait to capture on d5.

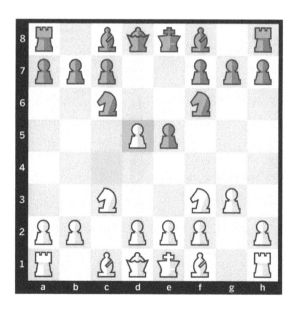

13. Caro-Kann Defense, page 106

Answer: 4 . . . Bf5. In the Classical, the bishop develops and attacks the knight (after you've traded pawns on e4, and the knight has just captured back on e4). In the Advance, you develop your bishop to f5 on move 3. It's one of the few openings that develops a bishop before a

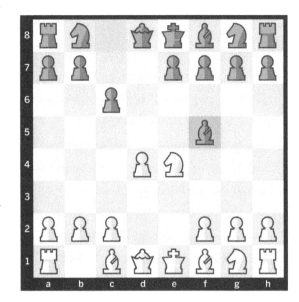

knight, but the idea is that this bishop must develop before placing a pawn on e6, which would block it in.

14. Scotch Opening, page 107

Answer: 3. d4 is the next move in the Scotch, offering an immediate pawn trade in the center. Black will capture, and white takes back with the knight.

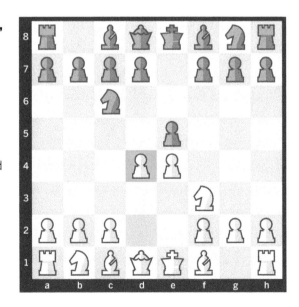

15. Fried Liver Attack, page 107

Answer: 6. Nxf7 any way, sacrificing the knight to bring the king out, and after the king captures your knight (6 . . . Kxf7), you play 7. Qf3 with a fork on the king and knight on d5. White is in a much better attacking position, and black is in danger of quickly getting mated if they retreat

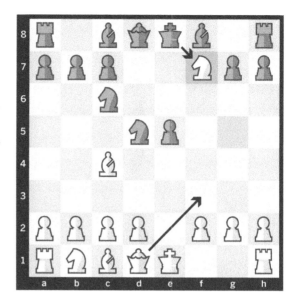

to g8. The only way to save the knight is with 7 . . . Ke6, but bringing the king to the center of the board is extremely dangerous.

16. Scholar's Mate, page 108

Answer: White is threatening 4. Qxf7#. Black should play either 3 . . . Qe7 or 3 . . . g6. The queen will protect the f7 square again, and . . . g6 will block the queen's path and kick her away.

17. London System, page 108

Answer: Castling is delayed because the pawns are not traded (opening files) in the center. On move 2, white can play Bf4 before bringing a pawn to e3, which would lock in the dark-squared bishop. White can also play 2. Nf3 and then Bf4 next turn as in the diagram to the right.

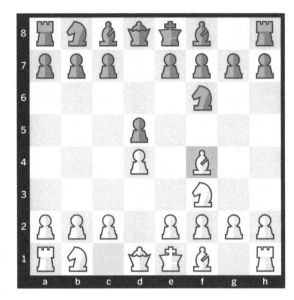

Because it's a system, these moves appear interchangeable; however, despite 2. Nf3 occurring more frequently, current theory states that 2. Bf4 is slightly more accurate.

18. Tarrasch Defense, page 109

Answer:
3 . . . c5 attacks the center again with a pawn. After the Main Line, 4. cd ed, black has the pawn wall for now.

19. Scandinavian Defense, page 109

Answer: 3 . . . Qa5. Occasionally, she might go to d6, but never play 3 . . . Qc6? or you will lose the queen to 4. Bb5!

20. Pirc Defense, page 110

Answer:
3 . . . g6 prepares to fianchetto the bishop to g7, which will aid in the attack on the center. Black will castle before striking in the center with a pawn.

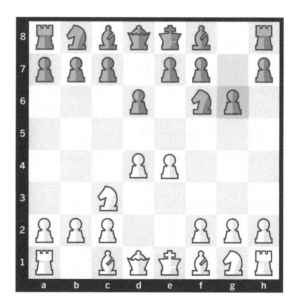

Resources

The following is a list of books, websites, and apps that will help you on your journey toward opening mastery. This list is not exhaustive, and it does not include books on specific openings, which you may be interested in as you define your opening repertoire.

BOOKS

Action Chess: Purdy's 24 Hours Opening Repertoire by C.J.S. Purdy

The Chess Advantage in Black and White by Larry Kaufman

Chess Openings for Black, Explained by Lev Alburt, Roman Dzindzichashvili, and Eugene Perelshteyn

Chess Openings for White, Explained by Lev Alburt, Roman Dzindzichashvili, and Eugene Perelshteyn

Chess Openings: Traps and Zaps by Bruce Pandolfini

Chess Openings: Traps and Zaps 2 by Bruce Pandolfini

Complete Defense to Queen Pawn Openings by Eric Schiller

Concise Chess Openings by Neil McDonald

Hypermodern Opening Repertoire for White by Eric Schiller

Logical Chess: Move by Move by Irving Chernev

Nunn's Chess Openings by John Nunn, Graham Burgess, John Emms, and Joe Gallagher

Winning Chess Openings by Bill Robertie

WEBSITES

365Chess.com

Chess.com

Chess24.com

ChessBase.com

ChessGames.com

ChessKid.com

Lichess.org

USChess.org

APPS

Chess (from Chess.com)

Chessable

ChessKid

Kasparovchess

Magnus Trainer

ACKNOWLEDGMENTS

Thank you to Danny Rensch and Mike Klein of Chess.com and ChessKid
.com for publishing so many of my articles, several of which informed this
book. Love and appreciation also go to my son for understanding that
"Mom has to work on her book!" Thanks to my students, whose interest
in and excitement about chess generates enthusiasm all around. Finally,
I'm grateful for the keen eye of editor Van Van Cleave, whose collabora-
tive efforts allowed me creativity while keeping me concise.

ABOUT THE AUTHOR

Jessica Era Martin has been a chess instructor for
twenty years and has coached teams in three states
at the state and national championship levels. Jessica
achieved her MFA from Queens University in Charlotte
and is the past Vice President of Scholastic Chess with
the North Carolina Chess Association. Jessica is the
founder of Over the Chessboard, an organization dedicated to promoting
chess for everyone, and a scholarship has been created in her name at
the International School of Tucson. She is also the author of *How to Play
Chess for Kids, My First Chess Book*, reprinted in 2021 as *Learn to Play
Chess*, and *Chess Strategy for Beginners*. Jessica is a mother, poet, and
avid table tennis enthusiast.

CPSIA information can be obtained
at www.ICGtesting.com
Printed in the USA
BVHW010255120423
662148BV00005B/152